Practical Anonymity

Practical Anonymity
Hiding in Plain Sight Online

Peter Loshin

ELSEVIER

AMSTERDAM • BOSTON • HEIDELBERG • LONDON
NEW YORK • OXFORD • PARIS • SAN DIEGO
SAN FRANCISCO • SINGAPORE • SYDNEY • TOKYO
Syngress is an imprint of Elsevier

SYNGRESS.

Publisher: Steve Elliot
Development Editor: Benjamin Rearick
Project Manager: Mohana Natarajan

Syngress is an imprint of Elsevier
225 Wyman Street, Waltham, MA 02451, USA

First published 2013

British Library Cataloguing-in-Publication Data
A catalogue record for this book is available from the British Library

Library of Congress Cataloging-in-Publication Data
A catalog record for this book is available from the Library of Congress

ISBN: 978-0-12-410404-4

For information on all Syngress publications
visit our website at **www.syngress.com**

This book has been manufactured using Print On Demand technology. Each copy is produced to order and is limited to black ink. The online version of this book will show color figures where appropriate.

Working together
to grow libraries in
developing countries

www.elsevier.com • www.bookaid.org

CONTENTS

Google CEO Eric Schmidt ignited a firestorm in 2009 when he declared "Privacy is dead." He said:

> If you have something that you don't want anyone to know, maybe you shouldn't be doing it in the first place, but if you really need that kind of privacy, the reality is that search engines including Google do retain this information for some time, and it's important, for example that we are all subject in the United States to the Patriot Act. It is possible that that information could be made available to the authorities.

For those with legitimate reason to use the Internet anonymously—diplomats, military and other government agencies, journalists, political activists, IT professionals, law enforcement personnel, political refugees, and others—anonymous networking provides an invaluable tool, and many good reasons that anonymity can serve a very important purpose.

Anonymous use of the Internet is made difficult by the many websites that know everything about us, by the cookies and ad networks, IP-logging ISPs, and even nosy officials may get involved. It is no longer possible to turn off browser cookies to be left alone in your online life.

For many, using any of the open source, peer-reviewed tools for connecting to the Internet via an anonymous network may be (or seem to be) too difficult, as most of the information about these tools is burdened with discussions of how they work and how to maximize security. Even tech-savvy users may find the burden too great—but actually using the tools can be pretty simple.

For many users, being able to use the Internet anonymously can literally be a matter of life and death, so no one should be prevented from using anonymity tools because they can be too confusing—particularly if the need is urgent. This book will provide the know-how to get vulnerable users online, anonymously, as quickly and safely as possible.

Read on to discover how to use the most effective and widely used anonymity tools—the ones that protect diplomats, military and other government agencies, journalists, political activists, law enforcement personnel, political refugees, and others. This practical guide skips the theoretical and technical details and focuses on getting from zero to anonymous as fast as possible.

ACKNOWLEDGMENTS

I would like to thank all those who have contributed to the Tor Project for their important contributions to this important enterprise. In particular, I want to express my gratitude to those people connected with the Tor Project who were kind enough to help me complete this project:

Karsten Loesing, Metrics Researcher and Project Manager, who was kind enough to find time in his busy schedule to review this book for technical correctness.

Runa A. Sandvik, Developer, Security Researcher, and Translation Coordinator, who was gracious and helpful in answering some of my peskier questions about Tor—and shared some insights into the difficulties of writing about Tor.

Roger Dingledine, Project Leader and one of the original developers of Tor, who very patiently spent close to an hour explaining to me how Tor works at the 2013 Tor Project hack day in Boston.

Andrew Lewman, Executive Director, without whose assistance I would not have been able to complete this project.

As always, I am grateful for the skilled professionals at Elsevier, starting with Syngress publisher Steve Elliot who convinced me to start writing books again, and Ben Rearick, Editorial Project Manager, and Mohana Natarajan, Production Manager, who helped guide the whole project to completion.

CHAPTER *1*

Anonymity and Censorship Circumvention

Despite appearances, the Internet is not now (nor has it ever been) an anonymous medium. People often *behave* as if they are anonymous, for example, by posting obnoxious comments on websites or browsing objectionable content with a browser's "incognito" or "private browsing" modes.

However, whenever you connect to the Internet you are announcing your identity through your computer's Internet Protocol (IP) address, which identifies you: through your Internet service providers (ISPs) account to find your home address, or through your company's network to identify your computer at work.

When you connect to the Internet from someone else's IP address (e.g., from a hotel wi-fi account, a computer cafe, or a borrowed PC), you can still be identified by anyone monitoring your session when you log in to social networking sites or check your webmail.

People continue to discover that using the Internet leaves forensic evidence—evidence which, if someone wants it, can be easily collected and linked to you. Given the revelation in June 2013 of the PRISM program, under which the National Security Agency (NSA) was working with nine of the biggest providers of Internet services (including Google, Microsoft, Apple, Facebook, and several others) to collect and store data, concerns about privacy protection—including in the US—are far from paranoid fantasies.

An excellent illustration of this was played out in 2012 by former CIA Director David Petraeus (and friends) who famously had their private e-mails made public. If the director of the CIA lacks the tradecraft to cover the digital traces of his extramarital affairs, what hope have others? (See "Don't be a Petraeus: A Tutorial on Anonymous Email Accounts" at https://www.eff.org/deeplinks/2012/11/tutorial-how-create-anonymous-email-accounts.)

The Petraeus example shows that even when using borrowed network connections, spread across different locations, the typical user exposes enough personal information to make any pretense of online anonymity a sham.

Anything you do online is susceptible to numerous attack vectors, but it is possible to cover the most obvious of your tracks, if you are careful. That is the subject of this book: how to connect to the Internet with the confidence that someone listening in to your connection won't be able to figure out what you are doing (or at least make it very difficult).

The other side of Internet anonymity is censorship circumvention. There are many Internet users who live in countries like China or Iran where national firewalls restrict access to websites deemed unacceptable to the ruling parties. These users would probably willingly trade the nuisance of targeted marketing (one of the reasons some people use Tor in more liberal countries) for the ability to bypass national web censorship—but they don't have to, because if you can connect to the Internet anonymously, you can usually also bypass the censors.

How can citizens living under repressive regimes read uncensored news when their governments filter all Internet access? How can diplomats, spies, business people, journalists report the full truth on conditions in places where Internet access is monitored for political or corporate advantage, or filtered for undesirable content? How can whistle-blowers or police informers provide information on wrongdoing without exposing themselves to personal danger?

The answer for many is to use Tor (https://www.torproject.org), an open source project whose goal is to allow users anywhere to use the Internet, anonymously and without limitation by censors. Tor protects anonymity by reducing the ability of adversaries to extract personally identifiable information by performing network traffic analysis.

By "adversary," I mean whoever is trying to find your identity and location, whether a government agency, a corrupt official, a manager, or a stalker. And by "traffic analysis," the Tor Project explains in "Why we need Tor" (https://www.torproject.org/about/overview.html):

Using Tor protects you against a common form of Internet surveillance known as "traffic analysis." Traffic analysis can be used to infer who is talking to whom over a public network. Knowing the source and destination of your

Internet traffic allows others to track your behavior and interests. This can impact your checkbook if, for example, an e-commerce site uses price discrimination based on your country or institution of origin. It can even threaten your job and physical safety by revealing who and where you are. For example, if you're travelling abroad and you connect to your employer's computers to check or send mail, you can inadvertently reveal your national origin and professional affiliation to anyone observing the network, even if the connection is encrypted.

How does traffic analysis work? Internet data packets have two parts: a data payload and a header used for routing. The data payload is whatever is being sent, whether that's an email message, a web page, or an audio file. Even if you encrypt the data payload of your communications, traffic analysis still reveals a great deal about what you're doing and, possibly, what you're saying. That's because it focuses on the header, which discloses source, destination, size, timing, and so on.

A basic problem for the privacy minded is that the recipient of your communications can see that you sent it by looking at headers. So can authorized intermediaries like Internet service providers, and sometimes unauthorized intermediaries as well. A very simple form of traffic analysis might involve sitting somewhere between sender and recipient on the network, looking at headers.

But there are also more powerful kinds of traffic analysis. Some attackers spy on multiple parts of the Internet and use sophisticated statistical techniques to track the communications patterns of many different organizations and individuals. Encryption does not help against these attackers, since it only hides the content of Internet traffic, not the headers.

More About Tor

Who Is the Tor Project

"Due diligence" is a fancy way of saying, "do your homework before taking a risk." Any time you use a piece of software to protect your privacy or security, you must trust the authors and publishers of that software. You should have confidence that the people who make that software available are both skilled and trustworthy.

They should be skilled, so you don't have to worry about excessive bugs in production software, or that easily found bugs will go unfixed for very long.

And they should be trustworthy, so you don't have to worry about developers giving in to pressure from anyone to modify the software in a way that reduces the user's security.

Trust in people you don't know personally usually derives from those people's reputations. The Tor Project has a reputation for openness and transparency: much of their business, from tracking bugs to long-term project development to discussion of how best to fulfill their functions, is done in the open, on their wiki, in their discussion lists, and on their website. All source code of their software, as well as the source code to their website, is accessible for review and comment.

More important even than learning how the Tor protocols work, if you want to rely on Tor to protect your anonymity, you should learn more about the people behind Tor. Links to information about who is behind the Tor Project, financially and technologically, are provided in Section C.2 of Appendix C. The reader is urged to do his own research, as well.

1.1 WHAT IS ANONYMITY

Computers make anonymity much more difficult and complicated. Before computers and the Internet, simply blending in—making an effort to look and act like everyone else—would be enough to stay under the radar of anyone who might be looking for you, whether they are "the authorities," a bill collector, or a pushy salesman.

With computers, however, there are many different ways you can be identified—and they can all be automated, so there is no possibility of sneaking past a napping security guard or distracted secretary:

- IP address. All devices that connect to the Internet are identified by an IP address. IP addresses are assigned by the ISP and, given an IP address the ISP can identify the account and location of the system being used.
- Browser cookies. Web servers, especially those providing services, set "cookies" containing identifying information on your system when you access the service.
- System profiling. Information about your system, such as the browser you are using, your operating system, installed fonts, plugins, and other software (and more), can all be used to profile your system. For more about system tracking, see Panopticlick (https://panopticlick.eff.org/), a research project of the Electronic Frontier Foundation (EFF) (https://www.eff.org/).

You can't just surf into a website without giving away your identity, and if someone is looking for you (or your computer), they can use software that detects your access and notifies them immediately. There's no "sneaking in" on the coattails of a group of authorized users, no "social engineering" of gatekeepers in some other way, and no "hiding" in a crowd of IP addresses.

1.2 WHAT IS TOR

Tor is an anonymity and censorship circumvention tool: it is a suite of software that uses anonymizing protocols designed to work over ordinary IPs. Tor nodes (computers running Tor networking software) build safe network circuits between the user seeking anonymity and the websites the user wants to access. Tor clients use intermediary systems called "relays," computers that run Tor software and configured to create these circuits for anyone who needs them.

More About Tor

Getting the Details About Tor Network Protocols

This volume contains only a very general description of the way Tor works; it does not delve into all of the details of the protocol implementation. When I say that a Tor client makes a connection or circuit, you can assume that it includes a full measure of cryptographic exchanges to validate system identities, encrypt network data appropriately, and, basically, avoid doing anything that would expose the user and doing everything possible to prevent exposure.

For a fuller understanding of the Tor protocol, you can start with the protocol design document, "Tor: The Second-Generation Onion Router" (https://svn.torproject.org/svn/projects/design-paper/tor-design.pdf), which describes many of the security issues and challenges that must be addressed by an anonymity networking protocol. The actual protocol specification is also available, "Tor Protocol Specification" (Roger Dingledine and Nick Mathewson) at https://gitweb.torproject.org/torspec.git?a = blob_plain;hb = HEAD;f = tor-spec.txt.

Tor builds on the basic premise of a network proxy: a mechanism through which you can connect to a network, where the proxy system acts on your behalf. In other words, if you connect to a remote server through a proxy, the proxy connects to the Internet for you, and pretends to be you, for the purpose of connecting to that server—the server thinks that *you* are the proxy system, and doesn't know where you are actually connecting to the Internet from.

Proxies are great for circumventing rules imposed on your access to the Internet, whether those rules are imposed in the form of a national firewall, a corporate firewall, or parental control software. For example, a company that forbids its employees from using Facebook is able to enforce that prohibition by blocking all attempts to access the "facebook.com" domain from any system inside the corporate network, as well as anyone attempting to connect to an IP address associated with Facebook servers.

Employees can bypass this block by using a proxy service: another server, not blocked by the corporate firewall, accepts a URL from the blocked user, and then forwards content from the forbidden site to the user. Since the forbidden site is never directly accessed through the corporate firewall, it is not blocked.

Real proxies are a bit more complicated, and countermeasures can be used to disrupt or prevent access to proxies. Usually, this kind of proxy service is easily defeated by adding its address to the list of addresses blocked by the corporate firewall—and proxies can be discovered if IT staff notice increased use of bandwidth to connect to the proxy server. At that point, firewall rules can be modified to block access to the proxy server—and users are forced to find another proxy server, or some other means of bypassing the filter.

Simple proxies solve the problem of accessing content without limits or censorship for some users (for example, children who wish to bypass parental control software), but they fail in other cases, for example:

- You must trust that whoever runs the proxy server will respect your privacy, because the proxy server can see what websites you access and can log that information. If your adversary is able to get access to the proxy server, or is able to monitor your network sessions over the proxy server's Internet connection, your sessions are no longer private.
- Proxy servers are easily blocked, once they are detected—and they are not difficult to detect, especially as more people use the same proxies.

Tor is a more sophisticated form of proxy, because it more completely obscures your actual destination, and it doesn't always use the same destination address for anonymous traffic—which would make it identifiable, and therefore blockable by a firewall. (Some adversaries block Tor relays, because their addresses are openly available, making it necessary to use bridge relays and other mechanisms, to be discussed in Chapter 4.)

Instead of connecting to a proxy server and telling *it* what Internet server you want to reach, you connect to one Tor *node* and have it pass your traffic along to another Tor node. Tor nodes that are able to accept Tor traffic and forward it to their nodes are also known as *relays*. A Tor node that accepts traffic from another Tor node is called a *transit node*.

The Tor transit node your Tor client connects to has no idea of where your traffic is going—and this transit node can have no idea of where you are trying to connect, either. Only the Tor *exit node*—a Tor relay that forwards traffic from within the Tor network to the public Internet—knows where you are trying to connect, but it doesn't know where that traffic comes from.

When you connect to the Tor network, your computer chooses a random path through the network, picking a transit node to enter the Tor network, another transit node inside the network, and exit node, to forward your anonymized traffic onto the public Internet. The transit node you enter by can identify your computer's IP address and the IP address of the next transit node your computer has chosen for the circuit, but that is all.

The second-hop transit node, in turn, knows nothing about you or your intended destination—just the entry and exit nodes. And the exit node knows nothing at all about your system or your IP address, only the destination you want to reach. See Figure 1.1 for an overview of the Tor network.

Figure 1.1 gives a broad overview of how Tor works: the client, on the left of the image, picks out three Tor relays (shown inside the Tor network cloud), and creates successively encrypted tunnels that are peeled away at each relay, until the web session is opened through the exit node.

●●●————————————————————————————————

More About Tor

Visualizing the Tor Network

Graphically representing the different aspects of the Tor anonymizing network is not an easy task. Other images are provided later on in this chapter (see Figures 1.2 and 1.3), as well as links to other graphical representations. See the interactive graphic on the EFF page "Tor and HTTPS" (https://www.eff.org/pages/tor-and-https) for an excellent (animated!) illustration.

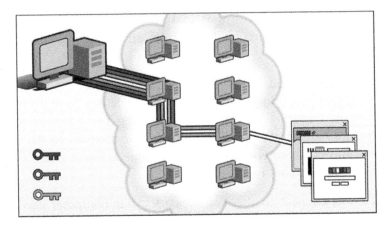

Figure 1.1 Tor clients encrypt data three times, once for each relay passing that data to its destination. Tor Project, https://www.torproject.org/dist/manual/short-user-manual_en.xhtml.

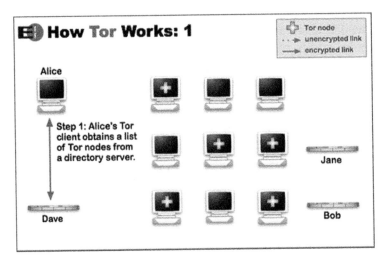

Figure 1.2 "Alice" is a person using a Tor client to connect to a Tor directory server running on the computer named "Dave."

For a discussion of some of the issues, plus some suggestions for more accurate/engaging visualizations of Tor for less-technical users, see "Visual overview of the Tor network" (https://blog.torproject.org/blog/visual-overview-tor-network).

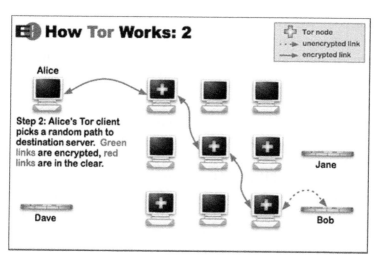

Figure 1.3 Encrypted connections are solid lines, plaintext connections are dotted lines.

1.3 WHY USE TOR

There are many good reasons to use Tor, many of which are detailed on the Tor Project website. Ultimately, the best reason for *you* to use Tor is your business. If you're not sure why you should consider using Tor, read on.

The two fundamental uses for Tor are to maintain privacy and to circumvent censorship.

There are many good reasons to stay private, mostly to avoid unwanted attention to your interests, whether that attention manifests itself with endless advertisements targeted to you based on your Google searches, or to avoid attention from network administrators monitoring traffic for "forbidden" content.

Privacy is implied in the right to be left alone. Given the amount of data that can be—and is—collected any time you connect to popular websites, it is reasonable to avoid leaking personal information. To see just how much of your personal information can be leaked, see Firefox Collusion (http://www.mozilla.org/en-US/collusion/), an add-on for Firefox that graphically demonstrates how much information is gathered by various advertising networks.

Also, see Disconnect (https://disconnect.me/tools), an anti-tracking browser extension for Chrome which "disconnects" Google, Twitter, and Facebook logins so they don't stay active and collect your information after you leave their sites. As they say in their code repository, "Disconnect stops third parties and search engines from tracking the web pages you go to and searches you do."

One proposed solution to the privacy problem is the "Do not track policy" (https://www.eff.org/issues/do-not-track), referring to a proposed "Do not track (DNT) header" for HTTP, that would be used to indicate a user request to disable tracking of the user's activities by the remote web server and/or third-party tracking. The problem with this "solution" is that it depends on servers honoring the request—which is just that, a request. There is no way to enforce compliance with the request, and doing so would harm the business model of the companies who most often do tracking. See also "Do Not Beg: Moving Beyond DNT through Privacy by Design" (http://www.w3.org/2012/dnt-ws/position-papers/21.pdf), which explains why DNT is a nontechnical nonsolution to a problem that Tor solves.

Using an anonymizing network like Tor gives users control over what information is revealed through their own browsing.

If the remote server or network connectivity provider is not aware of the actual location or organization of the user browsing anonymously, that server cannot tailor their replies based on that information.

This is one way countries maintain "great firewalls" to cut off their citizens from access to news sources considered harmful to the regime.

Corporate websites can tailor offers specifically to a user depending on whether they are already a customer; they can also be configured to prevent information gathering on the part of competitors ("does Gimbels tell Macys?"). Likewise for the activities of undercover law enforcement agents, who could tip off network-savvy criminals who can trace their online activity to IP addresses assigned to law enforcement agencies. These examples are not just possibilities, but actual documented facts.

Not every need for privacy requires the same solution. For example, as noted, sometimes just using a proxy service of some sort will provide a suitable and sufficient solution. Likewise, a person who just wants to conceal their browsing history from a spouse can use a "private browsing" (Firefox) option in their browser ("Incognito browsing" in Chrome) if they are planning a special surprise gift or party, and don't want their spouse to know what websites they've been visiting.

Using private browsing does NOT offer any kind of real anonymity: someone monitoring your network or accessing server logs at the sites you access will still know all about you. These private browsing options are strictly to conceal your web activity/history from others with casual access to the same computer.

However, there is a great deal of difference between the privacy and anonymity needs of a person who wants to surprise a spouse and the needs of an activist working behind a national firewall. The latter faces an adversary that controls or can control every aspect of network computing in the country, and that has allocated significant human and equipment resources to further the cause of denying the activist Internet tools for organizing and resisting.

Assessing threats is an important activity, and is critical to the effective use of any kind of computer or network security tool.

Tor can be helpful to people who want to search for information about an embarrassing health condition without being spammed by Google Ads for products related to that condition. More than that, Tor can be a lifesaving technology—however, the greater your need for protection, the greater your need to gain a deep understanding of how Tor works and what it can and cannot do for you.

There are different ways to assess threats, particularly in regard to government agencies and other organizations. For example, the paper "How Do You Assess Your Organization's Cyber Threat Level?" (http://www.mitre.org/work/tech_papers/2010/10_2914/10_2914.pdf) describes, systematically, methods for determining how to decide on how worried you should be for your organization, depending on what you know about your adversaries.

Tor can help you if you need to use the Internet from a country where Internet users are punished for gathering (or disseminating) certain types of information.

To better understand just what kind of risks you face when using the Internet in the US, see EFF's "What Can the Government Do?"

(https://ssd.eff.org/your-computer/govt) for details about what rights you have in the US, and what the government can do while still honoring those rights.

Government agencies don't even need to monitor Internet transmissions themselves, if they are able to pressure ISPs and web publishers to maintain logs of all network activity. Most ISPs and websites spell out in their end user license agreements (EULAs) that they will cooperate with legitimate requests from government and law enforcement agencies—even if it means decrypting your "private" data to do so.

Not all big Internet companies treat their users' privacy rights with the same respect; see the EFF report, "Who Has Your Back?" (https://www.eff.org/who-has-your-back-2013), to get some idea of which companies are willing to support their users' privacy rights, and what they are (and are not) willing to do to back that up.

1.4 WHAT TOR CAN'T DO

If you assume all your network traffic is (or may be) monitored—as you would do if you are accessing the web from inside a corporation or from inside a country that runs a national firewall—you can also assume that accessing a forbidden website may cause a figurative "red flag" to spring up on an official's desktop.

Tor is designed to help with this type of scenario—but it does not provide complete protection.

Tor circuits are defined from the connection to an entry transit relay, through the Tor network via another transit relay, to the exit relay. Each of these hops, from one relay to another, are all encrypted. However, the connection from the exit relay to the destination website is not encrypted by Tor. If someone is monitoring your destination website's network, they may be able to get your web sessions, unencrypted. See Figure 1.3, where the link between the Tor exit node and the server (named "Bob") is shown to be unencrypted. Ideally, that last hop would be encrypted, but that is not always the case. One partial solution to this problem is described in the sidebar, "HTTP Secure (HTTPS) and HTTPS Everywhere," later in this chapter.

Tor also will not save you if your adversary has hacked your computer. For example, installing malicious software or hardware that captures, stores, and forwards your keystrokes (a technique called *keylogging*), or by installing some other malicious software that either prevents you from accessing network resources or that records your activities. Remember, anonymity loves company.

See also the article "Anonymity Loves Company: Usability and the Network Effect," at (http://freehaven.net/anonbib/cache/usability:weis2006.pdf) for more about this phrase and its implications. You will not be particularly anonymous if you are the only person using Tor in a network, whether it is a corporate network isolated behind a corporate firewall or a national network isolated behind a national firewall.

Tor also cannot prevent you from compromising your own anonymity through your online activities. Accessing personal accounts over Tor, entering personal information on websites accessed via Tor, and opening files that you downloaded over Tor can all compromise your anonymity (see section "Don't open documents" for more details).

Tor also cannot protect you from an *end-to-end timing attack*, where the attacker is able to monitor your network traffic as it leaves your computer, as well as the traffic arriving at your intended destination server. In this case, your adversary would have to be able to monitor your outbound traffic—even if it is encrypted—as well as the ability to monitor the network traffic arriving at your intended destination. Such an attack is usually assumed to be possible only for an adversary with lots of resources and a high degree of access to many different networks—such an adversary is often assumed to be a nation state or similarly powerful entity.

To illustrate, consider this example: an attacker detects that you have sent out 100K of encrypted data to somewhere via a Tor (by monitoring your network transmission locally), and then detects, moments later, the arrival of 100K of data at an activist blog. This can spell trouble for the blogger, if it is detected, even if the data was encrypted, because your attacker can prove that it was *your* computer that was the source for forbidden content. It could be even worse, if an inflammatory article appears on the website immediately after the data arrives at the site. In either case, the user's anonymity is compromised, and the user should expect to be subject to additional scrutiny by the authorities.

Although the Tor Project developers continue to work on ways to minimize vulnerability to this type of attack—and even though this type of attack requires extensive resources and skill to be used successfully—you should be aware that it is possible, and take precautions. See "Avoid risk and protect online identity" (https://blog.torproject. org/blog/avoid-risk-and-protect-online-identity), for some articles about blogging safely, among other topics.

1.5 HOW TOR WORKS

Tor uses an "onion routing" protocol to allow users to access the Internet via a proxy network, and thereby prevent the destination server (or anyone monitoring the server or its network) from being able to identify the IP address of the user's computer. Onion routing is so-called because the network traffic is wrapped up in several layers, with systems at either end peeling away the layers as the traffic is sent and received—like an onion.

Tor's effectiveness depends on having many users from all over among whom you can "hide." The basic process can be summarized as follows:

- A Tor client gets a list of all available Tor relays. This list is called a consensus document, because it is the list of all Tor relays that the Tor directory servers can agree are connected and can be trusted to handle Tor traffic. See Figure 1.2.
- The Tor client creates its own path through the Tor network, consisting of an entry hop through a transit node, a second hop from the entry point to another transit node, and a third hop from the internal transit node to an exit node.
- The exit node, on behalf of the client, connects to the desired destination (usually a web server) and acts as a proxy for the originating Tor client. See Figure 1.3.

If you are observing the network traffic sent to and from the Tor client, you will be able to detect that the client is sending Tor traffic to a Tor entry node. That traffic (from the client to the Tor entry node) will be encrypted and can be considered private for all practical purposes (assuming that Tor has been installed, configured, and used correctly).

If you are observing the network traffic sent between the Tor client and the Tor exit node for that circuit, you may be able to detect the plaintext of the web session (see sidebar on HTTPS; if HTTPS is not being used to encrypt end-to-end), but you will still not be able to discover the location (IP address) of the originating Tor client.

See also this interactive graphic from EFF at https://www.eff.org/pages/tor-and-https for a graphical representation of the ways in which network traffic is protected, and which traffic is vulnerable, depending on whether you are using Tor, HTTPS Everywhere, or both.

●●● ───

More Tools for Tor

HTTP Secure and HTTPS Everywhere

HTTPS stands for "HTTP Secure" (HTTP = Hypertext Transfer Protocol); when used in a URL, it signals the web browser that the server is using an extra protocol (TLS, or Transport Layer Security) for encrypting web browsing data.

If you are browsing a website that supports HTTPS, all URLs will be prefixed by https:// (not http://), and all sent to or from the server will be encrypted so that only the receiving computer can decrypt it.

When HTTPS is *not* in use, an adversary monitoring your local network (e.g., wi-fi or Ethernet) can see what websites and what pages on those websites you are accessing, as well as what information you are sending and receiving, including user IDs and passphrases.

When HTTPS *is* in use, an adversary may be able to determine which website you are accessing, but they cannot see what pages you are using or what information you are sending or receiving.

HTTPS by itself is not enough to allow you to access a website anonymously, but it is an important method to reduce the amount of information you expose online.

The HTTPS Everywhere project (https://www.eff.org/https-everywhere) is a collaboration between the EFF (https://www.eff.org/) and the Tor Project. It is a web browser extension for Firefox/Chrome that makes it easier to use HTTPS on websites that support it. HTTPS Everywhere is incorporated into the Tor software distribution, and is recommended for all users who wish to prevent having their web sessions monitored and/or taken over by attackers.

1.5.1 Tor Protocol Components

The different systems involved in using Tor include:

- *Tor client*, software that runs on a computer (PC, netbook, tablet, phone, whatever) to use the Tor software to connect to the Tor anonymizing network. The system running the Tor client software is also referred to as a Tor client.
- *Tor directory service*, consisting of a number of servers that maintain a database of active Tor relays, and respond to requests for information about active Tor relays.
- *Tor entry node*, a system that accepts network traffic from Tor clients and forwards it to any other Tor node. The entry node can be any type of Tor relay (exit, transit, or bridge). Because Tor traffic is encrypted from the client to the first Tor network hop (the entry node), it knows only the IP address of the originating Tor client, but does not know the destination and it cannot access any of the content being transferred.
- *Tor transit node*, a computer that accepts Tor traffic from Tor nodes and forwards it to other Tor nodes. Tor transit nodes can be used to create either the first or second hop in a Tor circuit, and these nodes have no way to know where the network traffic they forward is destined or what is in the network traffic they are forwarding.
- *Tor exit node*, a computer that can accept Tor traffic from any other Tor node and forward it to its intended destination on the public Internet. Tor exit nodes may be mistaken for the source/destination of objectionable or suspicious content, and the exit node will have access to any unencrypted data transmitted by or to the Tor client. This is why it is important to use HTTPS Everywhere (see sidebar above).

Tor network nodes (systems that forward Tor traffic) are also referred to as *relays*. A Tor relay designated as an exit node can also be used as a transit node; the node type depends on context of how it is being used in a circuit, though Tor relay maintainers can set up their relays as exit relays or for transit (nonexit) use only.

Tor clients communicate directly only with the Tor directory service (to discover Tor relays) and with Tor entry/exit relays (for sending and receiving data). A Tor client communicates with other nodes (transit and exit nodes) and with the intended destination—but those communications all go through the entry node and are relayed from one node to another.

For detailed description of the Tor protocol, see the Git repository for the Tor Protocol Specification, by Roger Dingledine and Nick Mathewson (see https://gitweb.torproject.org/torspec.git?a = blob_plain; hb = HEAD;f = tor-spec.txt).

1.5.2 Building a Secure Tunnel with Tor Node Public Keys

Tor client randomly selects a route, picking one entry node, one transit node, one exit node, and then negotiates a circuit using those nodes.

The client encrypts whatever data it is sending to its destination (which, for greater safety, should be encrypted using the HTTPS protocol between the client and the remote server being accessed anonymously) using a key owned by the exit node it has chosen.

The client then encrypts THAT data with the transit node's key, and encrypts THAT data with the entry node's key. The Tor client is able to send and receive web data in a secure tunnel through the Tor anonymizing network:

- Tor entry node decrypts a packet and forwards it to the second-hop transit node;
- Tor transit node decrypts that packet and forwards it to the third-hop exit node;
- Tor exit node decrypts that packet and forwards it to destination.

A Tor transit node (or transit relay) can accept packets from any Tor client—so when it acts as the first hop in the Tor circuit, it is an "entry" node. However, any Tor transit relay can accept traffic from any Tor client, and forward it to any other Tor client (e.g., another transit relay or an exit relay).

Since entry nodes accept traffic from any Tor client, an adversary that observes a Tor client initiating a Tor circuit with the entry node knows with certainty only that that client is using Tor, and the entry node being used. The entry node will forward that client's traffic—as well as *other* clients' traffic, to Tor transit nodes. The adversary shouldn't be able to figure out which traffic goes to which transit node as long as there are enough other Tor users using the same entry relay.

The second-hop transit node forwards the traffic to the exit node—without knowing which Tor client's traffic it is carrying. The same goes for the exit node as long as HTTPS is being used (if the destination does not support HTTPS, the exiting traffic is in plaintext, and can be monitored).

As data is passed back and forth through the Tor network, the encryption layers are "unwrapped" like an onion (hence the name, "onion routing").

In this way, the only Tor node in the circuit that can be linked to the Tor client is the entry node; the only Tor node that can be linked to the destination is the exit node. The internal (second hop) transit node can be linked only to the entry and exit nodes—resulting in a communication circuit that effectively erases the link between the Tor client and the Internet server it is connecting to.

1.5.3 The Exit Node Acts on Behalf of the Tor Client

All network traffic exiting the Tor network looks as if it is entering the Internet from the Tor exit nodes—not from the original client nodes.

This is why the entire Tor network functions as a proxy: you put data in, and it repeatedly encrypts and repacks the data to make it look as if it is all coming from the exit node. Likewise, all inbound traffic appears to be coming from the client's chosen "entry" node, rather than from the actual (and perhaps blocked) server.

This is the property that makes Tor useful: when a national firewall is in place that blocks, for example, all traffic to YouTube, Tor users can bypass those blocks by using Tor entry nodes that have not been blocked by the national firewall.

For the same reason, Tor users can browse the Internet without giving away personal information (in particular, their IP address, which can be almost always be linked directly to a specific location).

1.6 WHO USES TOR

People use Tor for many reasons.

Some of those reasons might be considered "wrong" because they bypass controls placed on Internet access by various authorities: it could be a child accessing websites forbidden by parents, an employee accessing websites forbidden by management, or a citizen accessing websites forbidden by the government.

Tor allows users to access, and even publish, content on the Internet without having to be cleared by the authorities—and also in a way to avoid being detected and identified. The risk for a fractious child accessing a forbidden website may be (in some cases well-deserved) parental discipline, but for others, like a whistle-blowing employee or political activist, the risks can be higher—both to the whistle-blower who faces retribution and to the people who are denied access to the whistle-blower's information.

Tor gives these users a tool for doing good: reporting important information or organizing opposition to a repressive regime, for example. While there are many valid reasons to use Tor, some people see it as a threat that would allow criminals to commit crimes with impunity.

The problem with that argument is that anyone who is enough of a criminal to commit a crime *with* Tor can also accomplish the same goal of anonymity through other criminal means—like stealing someone else's phone or computer, or running botnets to control hijacked computers.

The argument also assumes that "wrong" and "illegal" are the same, when they clearly are not. The people who develop and support Tor do so because they believe strongly in human rights and the need for anonymity to protect those rights, particularly in situations where exercising those rights without anonymity would bring harm.

The Tor Project website has a great page that describes some of the people who use Tor (see https://www.torproject.org/about/torusers. html.en). This isn't an exhaustive list, but it is useful to consider that in any case where an otherwise law-abiding citizen wishes to avoid being identified by a government or other agency, Tor may be useful.

From the Tor Project website, here are some categories of users that will find Tor helpful.

1.6.1 Normal People
Your ISP—or people who work at your ISP—can see everything you do on the Internet. Maybe not all the details (if you are accessing

websites with HTTPS) but they can log every website and every web page you connect to, when and for how long. Web advertising networks can also track much if not most of your web activity. If you are accessing the Internet at work, your employer (and their ISP) can also keep tabs on what sites you are accessing.

Why is this a problem for "normal people"? For a number of reasons:

- Because it is very easy to jump to conclusions based on web activity. That may be as annoying as having advertisement networks popping up ads for products related to your most recent search engine queries, or as serious as losing a job if your employer assumes you have cancer because you googled "chemotherapy."
- Because marketers and others with access to web browsing records can use an IP address to map to a physical address, and link that with other information about you and your web activity.
- Because they wish to prevent children from giving away too much information online (see above).
- Because they want to research topics that are considered "sensitive" (for example, alcohol in Saudi Arabia or human rights in China), and those searching on sensitive topics are either blocked (censored) or flagged for investigation or other unwanted attention.

It should be noted that while your Facebook or Google account over Tor will protect you from someone intercepting your communications—but it will not protect you from an adversary like that described by the PRISM project run by the NSA, where the NSA has access to the Google or Facebook servers. Your personal data remains on those servers, stored subject to the websites' administrative policies.

In general, it is good practice to avoid using Tor to access any personally identifiable information about yourself *if doing so puts you at risk.*

1.6.2 Military
Tor was originally developed with funding from the US Naval Research Laboratory, with the intention to use Tor for protecting government communications. There are numerous military applications for Tor:

- Covert operations and field agents can use Tor to avoid detection by adversaries capable of monitoring network activity. Tor gives agents a tool for covertly connecting to systems known to be under the control of the military (IP address registration is public, including IP addresses assigned to governments and military).

- Hidden services (see Chapter 6, also sidebar "Tor Hidden Services") can be used to collect and disseminate information (for command and control functions) without revealing the location of the service and without revealing the location/identity of those using that service.
- Intelligence gathering, specifically connecting to resources used by an adversary. Using Tor, military personnel can connect to resources (web servers, online forums, etc.) without giving away their location/organization (which can be easily inferred from network client IP addresses).

Had the US government attempted to reserve Tor for only "official" uses, it would make Tor the opposite of anonymous: detecting Tor traffic would then become a foolproof method for identifying government actors.

1.6.3 Journalists and Their Readers/Viewers
Journalists, including bloggers and other citizen journalists, use Tor to protect themselves while reporting from parts of the world where there is no safe access to the Internet, as well as to protect their sources who wish to remain anonymous themselves.

1.6.4 Law Enforcement
Law enforcement officers and agencies can use Tor to further their investigations and operations. Tor can be used to:

- Gather information from questionable websites or network services maintained by or used for illegal activities.
- Run undercover operations without revealing that the systems being used are on IP addresses registered to law enforcement agencies.
- Help anonymous tipsters provide tips to law enforcement agencies without revealing their own identities.

1.6.5 Whistle-Blowers and Activists
Tor Project provides many examples of activists and whistle-blowers using Tor (see https://www.torproject.org/about/torusers.html.en#activists) to work for human rights and against corruption.

1.6.6 "High- and Low-Profile People"

Tor can be useful for anyone with a "high profile"—anyone who is active in the public sphere—to find a way to express (or investigate) opinions or issues that may be unpopular or unrelated to their public persona.

Likewise, Tor can offer those without many resources or power ("low profile") a way to express opinions or research issues that might be misinterpreted or that might cause them to be subject to unwanted attention. With Tor, they can express their opinions without fear of retribution or discrimination by employers, government aid agencies, or other authorities for holding the wrong opinions.

1.6.7 Business People and IT Professionals

Business people use Tor as an important tool for a number of purposes, including:

- Accessing competitors' online resources anonymously, especially when they use filters to censor the information that is provided to users who browse their websites from their rivals' networks.
- Providing truly anonymous options for employees to submit negative information to management.

IT professionals can use Tor as well, especially for testing corporate firewalls and other network resources. Because Tor traffic appears to be coming from outside the organization, it can be used to test company security/firewalls, for operational testing, and to bypass the corporate firewall without making any changes to the firewall.

1.6.8 Others

Anyone who wants to maintain a low profile and avoid being found can use Tor to their benefit. Whether you want to avoid an abusive family member, or an overzealous collections agency, Tor can help prevent abusers from locating their victims.

Tor is particularly useful for anyone in an asymmetric power struggle, where the user just wants to be left alone but their antagonist has access to sophisticated resources. For example, corrupt politicians, government employees, and law enforcement officers have been known to abuse their privileges.

1.6.9 The Benefit of Having Diverse Users

When they first learn about Tor, military and law enforcement users often express a wish that Tor either be made illegal or that there be a backdoor installed so that the "right people" be able to track down anyone using Tor for criminal acts.

However, a large part of Tor's usefulness is that there is no way to categorize "Tor users" as all being criminals (or spies or traitors). A Tor user may be a criminal, but she may also be a crime victim, or an undercover police officer, a diplomat, or an activist.

If, when Tor was being developed, the US Navy (or FBI or any other government agency) had decided that it should be classified and its use limited only to authorized government users—it would be next to worthless for maintaining anonymity. The reverse would be true, since any adversary monitoring a network would know for a certainty that the detection of any Tor traffic would identify the systems involved as being under the control of the US Navy (or other official agency).

Nor is there any reliable way to differentiate between the "good guys" and the "bad guys", making the existence of a backdoor a problem: how do you keep the bad guys from finding out about—and using—the backdoor? Especially given that sometimes the good guys can be fooled, coerced, or corrupted by the bad guys. So, there is no backdoor to Tor.

Having a diverse population of users, who can be confident that there is no backdoor, is what makes Tor useful because it allows everyone to hide more successfully.

●●●──

Tools for Tor

Tor Hidden Services

One byproduct of the Tor network architecture is that it allows the creation of *hidden services*: web or other network servers that are accessible only through the Tor network, and whose locations cannot be determined.

Here's how it works. Individual computers (nodes) can connect to the Tor network anonymously, and do anything that a regular Internet node can do. Usually, this involves accessing the web or other Internet services as a client—but a Tor node can also act as an anonymous server.

This means that the service can be accessed by anyone as long as they are using Tor, and that the hidden server can remain hidden (for the same reasons that Tor clients can remain hidden).

Hidden services are identified by so-called "pseudo-URLs," which look like standard URLs, but are identified by the pseudo-top level domain ". onion". A typical Tor hidden service resource might look like this:

```
http://idnxcnkne4qt76tg.onion/
```

This pseudo-URL is the official Tor Project website, accessible only by Tor as a hidden service.

1.7 HOW DO I USE TOR

Most people use the Tor Browser Bundle (TBB) to use the Tor anonymizing network. Using it is simple:

• Download the TBB (from https://www.torproject.org/), version appropriate for your operating system, and verify the download (see Appendix A).
• Extract TBB from the downloaded file, which for most users means clicking on the download file to open it.
• Run the Tor browser, which for most users means clicking on the Tor Browser application icon to start it.

The TBB runs all Tor software necessary to begin using the Internet anonymously, including initializing the Tor connection, opening the Tor Browser, and the Vidalia control panel to manage the Tor connection.

You may have trouble downloading the TBB in some parts of the world where the Tor website is blocked, but there are other ways to get the software, as described in Appendix B.

If you choose to use Tails, the process is slightly different:

• Download the Tails distribution (https://tails.boum.org), and verify (see Appendix A).
• Burn the Tails distribution to a bootable DVD.
• Boot Tails from the DVD.

Using Tails calls for a bit more tech savvy than the TBB because it must first be burned as a bootable DVD image, and the system on which it is to be run must be configured to allow booting from a disk.

Once Tails boots, you may also need to configure your network settings to connect to the Internet, but after the network connection is configured, Tails will automatically start the Tor-approved browser and you can begin anonymous browsing in the same way as when using TBB. See Chapter 2 for more details.

1.7.1 Plan Ahead and Learn Tor Now

Those three steps—download, extract, and run—should get most users started. If you want to know what the Tor Browser or Vidalia (the Tor control panel) looks like, or try out different websites, or connect to a Tor hidden service, this is all you need to know.

Many users will find this is enough to satisfy their needs based on their threat model. If your objective is preventing nosy neighbors from sniffing your web surfing sessions, this should be enough.

However, things can go wrong and there are a number of ways that you may inadvertently reveal your IP address or other identifying information even while using Tor. And of course, there are issues relating to using Tor in more demanding environments where your adversary has great access to systems and networks and there is more, and more active, monitoring activity.

Becoming familiar with Tor before there is an urgent need for it is a good idea, as a misstep under exploratory circumstances is far less dangerous than when there are actual dangers. So learn it now, before you need it, and when you need it you won't make any stupid mistakes.

1.7.2 TBB or Tails

Tor Project software is delivered in two forms: an executable file to run under the user's operating system of choice or an all-in-one package that incorporates the TBB client software in a stripped-down and "clean" version of Linux called Tails (https://tails.boum.org).

Tails includes most of the same components of the TBB as would be run under any other Linux distribution, but when burnt as a live-booting DVD (or USB drive), you can run Tails on any system that can be booted from a disk or thumb drive.

The differences between the two options (run on your own OS or run a separate OS) can be summarized in this way:

- TBB is more convenient and easier to use on my OS of choice.

- Tails can be made to be more secure and runs on any computer (that can boot from DVD or USB drive).

At this writing, Tails may be difficult or impossible to boot on OS X systems, so if you are using a Mac you will need to use the TBB.

1.7.3 Tor Browser Bundle
The TBB includes everything you need to begin browsing the Internet anonymously: the Tor network software as well as the Tor web browser (the browser is a modified version of Firefox). Versions of TBB are available for Windows, OS X, and Linux.

With TBB, you can run Tor from your normal desktop computer, at the same time as using non-Tor Internet access. This allows use on a computer that is using the Internet normally as well. It should not be a problem, but the user should be aware of proper security hygiene and best practices for security.

1.7.4 Tails
Unlike TBB, Tails is a complete secure operating system (based on Debian Linux) intended to be booted from a DVD or USB thumb drive. This allows use of Tor from Internet cafe computers, borrowed computers, or a computer that has been compromised at the OS level (e.g., keylogging software installed under Windows).

When properly authenticated, the user can be confident that the OS does not contain intentional backdoors and that the operating system will not record private information or allow remote websites to read or write personal data.

Tails is integrated with Tor, and (once a network connection has been configured) automatically starts the Iceweasel web browser and Tor.

1.7.5 What Can Go Wrong
Using Tor, or any software intended for security, means that you need to be able to trust that software. If you've decided Tor Project is a reputable and trustworthy group, you may also have decided to put your trust in their software. That's fine—but how can you be certain that the software you've downloaded is the same software that the Tor Project staff have published?

One way to increase trust is to download Tor directly from the Tor Project website (or a reliable mirror site). Their website uses HTTPS, so checking the URL in the address bar is a good idea: it should be the correct URL, and the padlock icon should show up as locked. This is a good indication the website has not been hacked, and the correct website is being accessed.

The best way to verify that the software you've downloaded is the same as that offered by Tor Project: all Tor software downloads (the TBB and Tails) are digitally signed, and the digital signatures are published on the same page as the software downloads.

To verify that the Tor software you've downloaded is the real Tor software, you'll need to download the signature file and use *OpenPGP* compatible software (see http://www.openpgp.org/) to validate the signature after importing the appropriate signing keys from a PGP keyserver.

Tor Project signing keys are available at the Tor Project website (https://www.torproject.org/docs/signing-keys.html) and instructions for validating downloads are posted as well (https://www.torproject.org/docs/verifying-signatures.html.en). Tor Project signing keys are also listed in Appendix A, as are instructions on how to validate Tor software.

Why all this extra work? One way to defeat Tor is to trick users into downloading a hacked version of Tor software rather than the real one. Such hacked software would appear to function as Tor software is intended, but might actually report Tor network activity directly to the adversary. This can be accomplished with a *man-in-the-middle* attack that intercepts the request to download Tor software, and returns hacked code rather than allowing the Tor Project website deliver the correct software.

1.8 USING TOR SAFELY

It's a good idea to heed the Tor Project warnings on how to use Tor safely (https://www.torproject.org/download/download.html.en#warning), but the warnings are summarized here.

1.8.1 Use the Tor Browser

Don't use other browsers; as browser features are added or changed, they may reveal more information about yourself than you would prefer. Rather than attempting to make all browsers safe for Tor, the Tor Project staff focus on making the Tor Browser as safe as possible.

1.8.2 Don't Open Documents

Don't open documents you downloaded via Tor on a computer that is connected to the Internet. This is very important though it applies only when using TBB; opening files with Tails is OK. Document files, such as .DOC or .PDF files, can cause trouble if they are opened by an application operating "in the clear." If a document has a web link inside, when the web content is downloaded (automatically) when opening the file, the link is opened by that application—not the Tor Browser. This is bad, because it reveals your IP address to the owner of the link. And, it's worse: an adversary could mark the URL in the document to link it to your connection when you downloaded the document—linking you definitively to the no-longer anonymous session you made, defeating your attempt at anonymity.

1.8.3 Don't Install or Enable Browser Plugins

Adversaries can use some plugins (like Flash, RealPlayer, Quicktime, for example) to force a system to reveal its IP address, thus defeating anonymity. Other plugins may have other weaknesses or malware, so it's best to simply avoid plugins entirely.

1.8.4 Avoid Websites that Are Not HTTPS-Enabled

Even with HTTPS Everywhere (which is incorporated in the TBB), if you are using a HTTP website, your session will be transmitted in the clear to the Tor entry node.

1.8.5 Use Bridges/Find Company

This is more a suggestion, but it applies to those who need greater safety. Because Tor network traffic is distinctive and can be identified by network monitoring software, the basic Tor setups described here may not be enough. Using the basic approach here described will leave you open to be identified as a user of the Tor network. In places where Tor is legal, this is not a problem, but elsewhere it may be. Tor bridge relays are special Tor relays that aren't publicly listed or easily discoverable. In places where national firewalls actively block access to Tor entry nodes, a bridge is a necessity. The suggestion to "find company" urges to try to use Tor in the context of many other Tor users with disparate interests, and in doing so making Tor user more "legitimate" because there are more different kinds of people using it.

CHAPTER 2

Using the Tor Browser Bundle

The Tor Browser Bundle is the Tor software suite used to run Tor from a desktop operating system (Windows, OS X, or Linux). To use Tor with the Tor Browser Bundle, you extract the compressed application after downloading it, and then click the Tor Browser icon to open an anonymous Internet session.

2.1 WHAT IS BUNDLED IN THE TOR BROWSER BUNDLE

The three major pieces of Tor Browser Bundle are Tor, Vidalia, and the Tor Browser; there are several other additional bits of code incorporated in the Tor Browser Bundle. This section describes the components of Tor Browser Bundle.

The Tor Browser Bundle is called a *bundle*, and the Torbutton software is a separate program because of legacy issues with the way Tor works: it used to be that you had to download different components of Tor software and use them together. Torbutton originally worked by giving the user a simple button that could be toggled to turn Tor browsing on and off from a web browser.

That is no longer the model for using Tor: you should probably never use Torbutton by itself, although Torbutton is still a separate program and is treated as a separate component of Tor Browser Bundle.

2.1.1 Vidalia

Vidalia is the control panel for Tor; it gives access to controls and configuration as well as things like a network map that shows what nodes are on the Tor network and which countries your Tor network circuits are transiting and also, seeing a graphic of network use, log of messages from Tor, etc.

It is completely possible to use Tor without ever using Vidalia, but it can be the best way to modify your Tor configuration, for setting up your node as a relay or bridge for other Tor users, or for setting up a

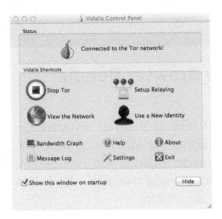

Figure 2.1 The Vidalia control panel includes a Status panel and shortcuts to Tor functions and configuration.

Tor hidden service. Vidalia is also used for network and advanced configuration functions such as:

- Setting up Tor to use a proxy service. Some users will need to configure Tor to use a proxy service; the proxy service may be required by the organization offering network access, or it may be necessary for the user to get through network restrictions on external network access. Tor can be configured to use the proxy service transparently to the end user.
- Getting through firewalls. Firewalls may filter network traffic based on the *port* being used. The port often identifies the type of networking service being used. Web traffic is usually on ports 80, 443, or 8080, and Tor can be configured to use those ports only in order to be passed through the firewall.

When starting Tor, Vidalia opens up a control panel window through which you may configure Tor, control the current Tor session, and access graphical representations of Tor-related data as well as Tor message logs, as shown in Figure 2.1.

●●●————————————————————————————————————

More About Tor

Vidalia's Future
Vidalia is currently used mostly within the Tor Browser Bundle (and a less-capable version in Tails), but moving forward within the Tor Project, Vidalia is considered a dead end. In the future, expect to see most of the functions handled by Vidalia to be incorporated elsewhere into the bundle

through the use of the Stem (https://stem.torproject.org/) toolkit for programming Tor in the Python programming language.

2.1.2 Tor

Tor is the core component that manages Tor network communication. This includes querying the Tor network for information about Tor relays, choosing entry, transit and exit relays and setting up Tor circuits, and all other Tor networking issues—but these networking functions are usually accomplished transparently to users.

The Tor software component manages Tor network communications in the same way that a Windows or OS X or Linux system includes networking software to do the same tasks of managing Internet connections with remote systems.

2.1.3 Mozilla Firefox ESR + Torbutton

The Tor Browser is actually a rebranded version of Firefox called Mozilla Firefox ESR (see http://www.mozilla.org/en-US/firefox/organizations/), a more stable release of the browser intended for use by groups or organizations that require less frequent updates and greater stability (ESR stands for "Extended Support Release"). See Figure 2.2.

The Tor Browser is configured to open a page at the Tor Project (https://check.torproject.org), that checks to see if your system is properly connected to the Tor network. This page "checks" the packets you've sent it to see whether you are connecting properly over Tor, and reports the result. It also displays the IP address that it appears you are using: if you are using Tor correctly, you will see a nice green banner, "Congratulations. Your browser is configured to use Tor" (see Figure 2.2). If you are not using Tor correctly, you will see a red banner indicating an error ("You are not using Tor").

As shown in Figure 2.2, the check.torproject.org page also displays the IP address that you appear to be using to connect. The check page verifies that the connection was made over Tor by comparing the IP address you appear to be using with the list of all valid Tor exit nodes; if there is a match, then the check page verifies that the network data is consistent with carrying Tor traffic.

Within the Tor Project is a standalone program, Torbutton (see https://www.torproject.org/torbutton/), which originally added an

Congratulations. Your browser is configured to use Tor.

There is a security update available for the Tor Browser Bundle.

Click here to go to the download page

Please refer to the Tor website for further information about using Tor safely. You are now free to browse the Internet anonymously.

Your IP address appears to be: **94.126.178.1**

This page is also available in the following languages:

العربية (Arabiya) Burmese Česky dansk Deutsch Ελληνικά (Elliniká) English español Estonish فارسی (Farsi) suomi français Italiano 日本語 (Nihongo) norsk (bokmål) Nederlands polski Português Português do Brasil română Русский (Russkij) Thai Türkçe українська (Ukrajins'ka) Vietnamese 中文(简)

Figure 2.2 The Tor Browser home page notifies you of the status of your Tor network connection. In this case, it indicates a good connection to Tor, but also a warning (in yellow) that an update to the Tor Browser Bundle is available (and should be downloaded).

actual button to an ordinary web browser; that button could then be toggled to turn Tor browsing on and off. All of the Torbutton functionality remains in the current Tor Browser Bundle, except that the button—to turn Tor anonymity on and off—is no longer present.

Although Torbutton is a separate program, it is integrated with the rest of the Tor Browser Bundle and it is recommended for most users to never use Torbutton separately from the browser. Torbutton functions are now managed through the Vidalia control panel or Tor configuration file.

By default, starting the Tor Browser will automatically turn on everything that needs to be turned on when using Tor—thus removing the need for a user-operating button to enable or disable it.

2.1.4 And More
The Tor Browser Bundle includes special patches to Firefox (see https://www.torproject.org/projects/torbrowser/design/#firefox-patches) to "enhance privacy and security." In addition, there are other tools that are incorporated in Tor Browser Bundle to enhance privacy and security, to keep data out of permanent storage, and modify the

information made available to external systems over the network (see https://www.torproject.org/projects/torbrowser/design/#components).

Other bundled components include:

- HTTPS Everywhere (https://www.eff.org/https-everywhere), already noted in Chapter 1, for secure browsing by encrypting web sessions between the client and the remote server. This protects data that would otherwise be transmitted in the clear before it arrives at a Tor entry node and after it is sent to the destination web server from a Tor exit node.
- NoScript (http://noscript.net), a browser plugin that prevents execution of untrusted scripts or programs. Such programs can be used by adversaries to manipulate browsers to betray their users in various ways.

2.2 USING TOR BROWSER BUNDLE

One of the first things you'll notice when first using Tor may be that it seems slow. This is due to the overhead of having Tor's three extra hops in each path, in each direction; performance is further impacted by having to encrypt (and decrypt) data at each Tor hop. Also a factor is that the amount of total bandwidth available to access the Tor network is limited and during times of high demand you may have to share that bandwidth with many other users.

The basics of using Tor, Vidalia, and the Tor web browser are similar—but not identical—whether you are using Tails or Tor Browser Bundle.

One difference occurs when using Tails on a system on a network that requires authentication (for example, if you have a wi-fi network that requires a passphrase). Tails is not configured for your system and network connection, so you'll need to configure the network connection manually, especially if a passphrase is required. (It is also possible to save Tails configuration when booting it from a USB drive, see Chapter 3 for more about *data persistence*.)

If the Tails system is connected to a wired network with no authentication required, Tails should boot correctly to the network and connect to Tor.

Another difference between Tor Browser Bundle and Tails is that in Tails, the rebranded version of Firefox is known as "Iceweasel." There is no functional difference between the two browsers. If you check the Help/About Iceweasel pulldown, you can see that the browser is, in fact, described as "designed by Mozilla," and follow the links for more information.

2.2.1 Getting it Started

Tor Browser Bundle can be installed on your hard drive, but this requires storing program and configuration files on the client system. Many users will prefer to keep Tor software on a removable drive.

After downloading the version appropriate for your operating system (and verifying the digital signature on the download), you unpack the software to the storage device or disk you prefer.

Extracting Tor directly into your Downloads directory is easiest, or you can specify a different directory or removable storage (like a USB thumb drive, removable disk, or other memory card) into which to extract the Tor Browser directory and files.

Using Tor from a removable drive gives you greater plausible deniability: having Tor installed on your computer is evidence that you may be using Tor—which may be considered evidence of wrongdoing in some places. Using Tor with removable storage means that you can remove the Tor disk or device and destroy or hide it.

2.2.2 Starting Tor Browser Bundle in Windows

The Windows download for Tor Browser Bundle is a self-extracting executable file; double-click it and Tor Browser Bundle files are extracted into a folder called "Tor Browser." To start Tor, open the Tor Browser folder and double-click on the file named "Start Tor Browser" (in some cases, this file may be named "Start Tor Browser. exe"). Vidalia will open, followed by the Tor Browser.

The Tor Browser should open at the check.torproject.org page (shown in Figure 2.2) with a "Congratulations" message plus the IP address that your Tor connection appears to be originating from (plus any other relevant messages).

2.2.3 Starting Tor Browser Bundle in Mac OS X

The Mac OS X download for Tor Browser Bundle is a zip file; double-click it and Tor programs are extracted into an OS X application folder named something similar to:

```
TorBrowser_en-US.app
```

The name will be different if you've chosen a different language version of Tor. To begin, double-click the icon named TorBrowser (as appropriate for the version you downloaded) and Vidalia will open, followed by the Tor Browser.

The Tor Browser should open at the check.torproject.org page (shown in Figure 2.2) with a "Congratulations" message plus the IP address that your Tor connection appears to be originating from (plus any other relevant messages).

2.2.4 Starting Tor Browser Bundle in Linux

These instructions should work for Linux, Unix, or version of the BSD operating system.

The Linux download for Tor Browser Bundle is a tar/gz file. With a user-friendly version of Linux such as Ubuntu, double-click the compressed download file. This opens an archive manager program to extract the compressed files.

Once extracted (either via command line or GUI), you should be able to double-click the "start-tor-browser" icon to run Tor. If the software was correctly extracted, you should see a prompt to either display the contents of the file, or to run it. Choose "Run" to start Tor.

For more details about installation, see below.

●●●———————————————————————————

More About Tor

Be Sure to Use Media Formatted for Linux

If you are having difficulty getting Tor to run on your Linux system from a USB drive, it may be due to the USB drive not being properly accessed by your Linux system.

Because you want to be able to run a program file from the removable media you installed Tor Browser Bundle on, that media must be formatted for use with Linux. If the media was formatted for some other operating system, you could have problems starting Tor, even after following all these directions.

To see if Tor is executable, check the first 10 characters listed at the left of the directory listing for each item in the directory. The first letter "d" indicates that the item is a directory; the letter "x" indicates that the item is "executable." If the media is not formatted in a Linux-friendly format, you will not see the letter "x" in the listing and you will not be able to run Tor.

When correctly installed, the listing for the Tor directory should look something like this (note the "x" in the listing for the "start-tor-browser" file):

```
$ ls -l
total 28
drwxr-xr-x 3 peter peter 4096 Apr  1 21:25 App
drwxr-xr-x 5 peter peter 4096 Apr  1 21:25 Data
drwxr-xr-x 5 peter peter 4096 Apr  1 21:25 Docs
drwxr-xr-x 3 peter peter 4096 Apr  1 21:25 Lib
-rwxr-xr-x 1 peter peter 7325 Apr  1 21:25 start-tor-browser
drwxr-xr-x 2 peter peter 4096 Apr  1 21:25 tmp
```

2.2.5 Installing on Ubuntu/GUI

Copy or move the Tor Browser Bundle download file to the desired location (either a directory/folder on the user desktop, or a removable drive, or other storage device).

Double-click the download file, and an Archive Manager window will open; click on the Extract button, and the Tor Browser Bundle will be extracted to the desired directory or device.

2.2.6 Installing on Ubuntu/Command Line

If you plan to use Tor from removable storage, first copy the compressed download file to the removable storage device (doing so with a GUI file manager is fine), and then switch to the Linux command line by opening the terminal program.

The first task is to change directory to the removable storage you are using; on Ubuntu, removable media are listed under the /media directory (other Linux distributions may use other directories or naming conventions), so change to that directory:

```
$ cd /media
```

Check the directory listing for the /media directory like this:

```
$ ls -l
total 36
drwx------ 12 peter peter 16384 Dec 31  1969 1E2C-46A0
drwx------  5 peter peter  4096 Apr 30 10:54 USB20FD
```

To install Tor Browser Bundle on the removable thumb drive named USB20FD, change to that directory like this:

```
$ cd USB20FD
```

Then, check the directory listing (assuming you've already copied the compressed Tor Browser Bundle file here) and it will look something like this:

```
$ ls -l
total 42876
-rw-r--r-- 1 peter peter  1303378 Feb 21 17:31 checkin.pdf
-rw-r--r-- 1 peter peter  2607996 Jan 18 22:38 IMG_0536.JPG
-rw-r--r-- 1 peter peter  3152669 Jan 18 22:38 IMG_0537.JPG
-rw-r--r-- 1 peter peter 36834876 Apr 29 14:43 tor-browser-
gnu-linux-i686-2.3.25-6-dev-en-US.tar.gz
$
```

Now, enter the following command to extract Tor Browser Bundle:

```
$ tar -xvzf tor-browser-gnu-linux-i686-2.3.25-6-dev-en-US.tar.gz
```

You will see every file being extracted, and then return to the prompt ($) when complete.

You should also know that Linux will autocomplete commands you enter for particular files, so you do not need to type out the entire filename, only enough to uniquely identify it in the current directory, then press the Tab key.

Check the directory listing one more time:

```
$ ls -l
total 42880
-rw-r--r-- 1 peter peter  1303378 Feb 21 17:31 checkin.pdf
-rw-r--r-- 1 peter peter  2607996 Jan 18 22:38 IMG_0536.JPG
-rw-r--r-- 1 peter peter  3152669 Jan 18 22:38 IMG_0537.JPG
drwx------ 7 peter peter     4096 Apr  1 21:25 tor-browser_en-US
-rw-r--r-- 1 peter peter 36834876 Apr 29 14:43 tor-browser-gnu-
linux-i686-2.3.25-6-dev-en-US.tar.gz
```

You will see a new directory named `tor-browser_en-US` (or other, for other languages). Change to the new directory:

```
$ cd tor-browser_en-US
```

and list the files in that directory:

```
$ ls -l
total 28
drwxr-xr-x 3 peter peter 4096 Apr  1 21:25 App
drwxr-xr-x 5 peter peter 4096 Apr  1 21:25 Data
drwxr-xr-x 5 peter peter 4096 Apr  1 21:25 Docs
drwxr-xr-x 3 peter peter 4096 Apr  1 21:25 Lib
-rwxr-xr-x 1 peter peter 7325 Apr  1 21:25 start-tor-browser
drwxr-xr-x 2 peter peter 4096 Apr  1 21:25 tmp
```

The file named "start-tor-browser" will start the Tor browser when you execute it from the command line like this:

```
$ ./start-tor-browser
```

2.2.7 Using Vidalia

Vidalia is the Tor control panel, meaning it gives the user tools to see how Tor is working and to manage Tor sessions. If you decide to set up a Tor relay, or to add a Tor hidden service, you would configure those through Vidalia.

●●●
───

More About Tor

Tails, Vidalia, and Configuration Persistence

The version of Vidalia included with Tails has fewer options than the version included with the Tor Browser Bundle, because many of Vidalia's configurable functions and features are related to setting up the computer as a Tor relay or a Tor hidden server.

Tails is designed for end users who need anonymity and a way to boot a system without leaving a forensic evidence trail. Although Tails can run as a relay or hidden service, it requires data persistence (see Chapter 3) and editing the Tor configuration file. Only experienced users should attempt to use Tails in this way.

To run a Tor relay or hidden server from a livebooting Linux distribution (like Ubuntu), one could boot the livebooting Linux and then run the Tor Browser from a USB drive (or recordable CD/DVD). The relay/hidden service could then be configured through the Tor Browser Bundle version of Vidalia.

───

The basic Vidalia interface is shown in Figure 2.1. The Status windows indicate whether or not Tor is running; when starting Tor a progress bar is displayed here. When the Tor software is up-to-date and the connection is fine, the status panel displays a green onion; any conditions that would make using Tor less secure are colored appropriately on the green/yellow/red "warning" scale.

2.2.8 Shortcuts

Tor shortcuts are listed here. *Help*, *About*, and *Exit* shortcuts should be self-explanatory; the Exit and Stop Tor shortcuts are not available in Tails because there is no other usable network connectivity under Tails. The Tails/Tor software is the only usable networking software in the Tails operating system, so there is no option to explicitly terminate Tor connectivity.

Vidalia's Help system is actually quite helpful, going beyond just telling you what to do in many cases, and providing explanations of why you would want/need to do something.

Also missing from the Tails version of Vidalia are shortcuts to set up as a Tor relay and access to Tor Settings. As noted, Tails is not meant to be used as a relay or hidden server but as a portable means to access the Internet anonymously: changing settings is possible but not recommended unless you know what you're doing. Also, if the Tails medium is not writeable (e.g., on a DVD-R), any changes to the configuration will not be saved for another session.

If you do need to edit the Tor configuration (in the file torrc), see this article describing how to do it: "Editing torrc from GUI" (https:// tails.boum.org/forum/Editing_torrc_from_GUI/).

2.2.9 Message Log

If you plan to use Vidalia (or manual methods) to change the Tor configuration or to modify how the current connection runs, you will want to check on your activity using the Vidalia message log.

Message log control buttons are at the top of the window, and you can choose to display the log in either Basic or Advanced modes.

In Basic mode, you get an overview of what's happening, similar to this message, which is the status displayed when Tor is started:

```
The Tor Software is Running

You are currently running version "0.2.3.25
(git-17c24b3118224d65)" of the Tor software.
```

In Advanced mode, you get many more protocol messages, with more details; for the same action (connecting to Tor) the Advanced mode displays much more information (see Figure 2.3).

You can also use the message log settings to change how to handle the message log, where to save it, and so on.

Not all log message text is visible when viewing the log in Vidalia, so it may be more convenient to save or copy messages and view them in a text editor.

2.2.10 Stop/Start Tor

This button does what it says: when Tor is running, it says "Stop Tor," and clicking it terminates the Tor networking software. When Tor is not running, it says "Start Tor" and clicking it starts the Tor software up again to restart Tor connectivity.

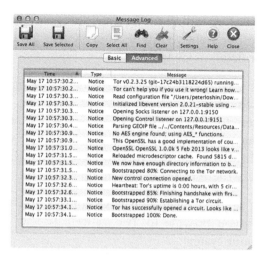

Figure 2.3 Advanced view of Tor message log. The contents can be searched, saved, copied.

Refer to Figure 2.1, where you can see that the status is "Connected to the Tor network!" and the first shortcut is labeled "Stop Tor."

2.2.11 Setup Relaying

By default, when you start Tor, you run as a Tor client: this means you can connect to the global (uncensored) Internet through the Tor network, or connect to hidden services. Your system to use Tor for its intended purpose: to bypass filtering, monitoring, and censorship.

Using Tor in this way consumes Tor network resources: entry and exit relays (because they place higher demands on their owners) are at a premium. As more Tor clients use the network, it is necessary for there to be more "infrastructure"—for the Tor network, much of the infrastructure is provided voluntarily, by users everywhere who have a bit of extra bandwidth and the desire to help out.

If you wish to help others who want or need to use Tor, you can do so currently by setting up your system to help provide Tor network infrastructure in three different ways:

- Non-exit relay;
- Exit relay;
- Bridge relay.

The implications of setting up as some kind of Tor network relay, and how to appropriately configure your system as a relay, are discussed in greater detail in Chapter 5.

Setting up as a relay, for those who understand and are willing to accept the consequences, is encouraged, as it is one of the simplest ways for Tor users to help contribute to Tor Project. However, setting up a Tor relay has some downsides, so if you are not willing to accept the (usually slight) risks but still want to help, a financial donation can be made to underwrite the cost of setting up relays.

When setting up as a relay, you have control over how much network bandwidth you provide to Tor as well as how network traffic passes through your system.

2.2.12 View the Network

Clicking on the "View the Network" button opens a window with four panels; working from the upper right corner and moving clockwise, these panels display the following (see Figure 2.4):

- Map of the world. When a Tor connection is selected, the map shows an approximation of the relays (by country) that each Tor connection transits. Location mapping is based on the country registered as using the IP address of those Tor relays; mapping precision is to country only, so relays in the same country will appear to be in the exact same spot.
- List of all currently active Tor relays, on the left side of the window. Relays can be sorted by the amount of bandwidth available (indicated by zero to three yellow bars, with more bars indicating greater bandwidth), by country, or by relay nickname. To get more information about a particular relay, click on it and details are displayed in the lower right corner of the window.
- Connection/status. This panel displays information about the Tor relays in use on all current Tor connections. Click on a connection and full details about the component relays are displayed in the lower right corner panel.
- Relay details. Displays the details of any one or more relays (either selected from the relay or the connection lists). Included are the relay location (country), IP address, available bandwidth, system uptime, and date/time the listing was last updated.

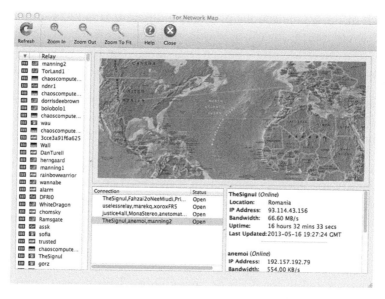

Figure 2.4 Tor network map display.

2.2.13 Use a New Identity

"Identity" in this case means the exit node on your Tor circuit that communicates directly with the remote servers you are accessing.

Why might you want to get a "new" identity? If you are accessing a personal e-mail account anonymously, and at the same time wish to publish content to an activist blog. Your e-mail account is not linked to anything—but if you use the same Tor circuit to update your activist blog, you risk having an adversary detect that the blog server and your e-mail server were used by the same Tor circuit. And now, your anonymity may be degraded because your adversary can determine that there is a connection between the two identities.

Unfortunately, this problem may not be solved using a new identity. Keep reading to understand (or, simply remember to reboot Tor/ Tails whenever starting a new anonymous task).

Tor sets up Tor network circuits (usually four new ones when Tor starts up), and seems to switch among them on a regular basis. Currently, the circuit will timeout after 10 minutes. Old circuits are discarded and new ones set up frequently enough to provide protection from adversaries that block the Tor protocols.

Each of those connections produces a different IP address representing your computer—in other words, a different identity. Clicking on the "Use a New Identity" button will cause Tor to switch to a new identity (usually, one that has already been set up but not yet used).

It is possible to modify how and how often Tor connections are used and timed out, as well as when to discard a connection that has already been used, by editing the Tor configuration file (torrc).

Clicking on the "Use a New Identity" button directs Tor to use a new identity for the *next* connection it makes. Tor *won't* drop a circuit and use a new one immediately, and the Tails documentation points out that "this feature of Vidalia is not a solution to really separate different contextual identities. Shutdown and restart Tails instead" (see https://tails.boum.org/doc/anonymous_internet/vidalia/index.en.html).

Also, as noted in the Tails documentation, Tails doesn't "magically separate your different contextual identities" (see https://tails.boum.org/doc/about/warning/index.en.html#identities), meaning this feature may not solve the problem you think it might. The best practice would be to restart Tails or Tor entirely.

2.2.14 Bandwidth Graph

Click on Bandwidth Graph to display a window that shows Tor network bandwidth, both for data transmitted and received, over time. This can be useful to check to see whether your system is actually connected to Tor and using Tor to transmit data, as well as to see how much data is actually being sent and received.

If you have set up your system to act as a Tor network relay, watching the bandwidth graph can give you some sense of how much (or how little) your relay is being used.

2.3 SETTINGS

Vidalia's Settings panel includes the following buttons:

- General
- Network
- Sharing
- Services
- Appearance

- Advanced
- Help

It is entirely possible to use Tor successfully and productively without ever having to change any settings—though not in all cases, including when using a proxy to access the Internet or when an adversary is blocking certain ports or blocking access to Tor.

●●●

More About Tor

Vidalia on Tails Is Missing some Features
The Tails version of Vidalia does not include a Settings panel, as the settings are used for configuring ongoing Tor usage (including configuration of hidden services and Tor relays), and Tails is primarily intended for simply connecting to the Tor network as an anonymous user.

2.3.1 General
The General settings include:

- An option to automatically start Tor network software when the Vidalia application opens. This option is recommended, and though not strictly necessary, it's a reasonable recommendation.
- Specifying where Tor software and related files are stored.
- Proxy application settings, including specifying the location and name of the proxy application, any options/arguments to use when starting the proxy, and a checkbox to turn it on.

If you are using a proxy application to connect to the Internet, it must be turned on to allow Internet access. Tor network access is accomplished over the Internet connection, so if connectivity from your network requires a proxy application, so does Tor connectivity.

2.3.2 Network
The Network settings refer to three issues related to network connectivity:

- Using a proxy to access the Internet. If you use a proxy to access the Internet, this is where you specify the network address and port of the proxy, your username and password, and specify the type of proxy being used (SOCKS4, SOCKS5, or HTTP/HTTPS).
- Accessing the Internet through a firewall that blocks some ports. Different network applications (e.g., the web, e-mail, chat, and so on)

use different ports to identify what kind of traffic is being transmitted; many firewalls block all ports except those used by the HTTP (web) traffic, ports 80 and 443. If there is no proxy and Tor is still not working, it may be because of a firewall; if so, try specifying only the two HTTP ports so all Tor traffic will be sent through them.

- Accessing the Internet through an ISP that blocks Tor connectivity. Some ISPs block Tor traffic by examining your network data and comparing IP addresses with the IP addresses of Tor relays (which are publicly available). This type of filtering may be a corporate decision, or it may be a policy enforced by a government. In either case, you will need to use a bridge relay (see Chapter 4 for more about Bridges).

If you are not sure whether or not you use a proxy, how the firewall works, or whether or not your ISP blocks Tor, be careful how you go about getting this information.

Asking IT or network staff about proxies, firewalls, and especially Tor connectivity, can be a red flag to those responsible for enforcing organizational networking policies.

You may not realize that a proxy or firewall is in use until you try unsuccessfully to connect to the Tor network. If possible, check your system's configuration yourself to see whether your operating system is set up to use a proxy. If there is no proxy but you still have trouble getting through to Tor, the firewall may be blocking access to Tor relays, so you can try using a Tor bridge (see Chapter 4).

If you need to check with support staff, seeming to be ignorant can be better than seeming to be devious. So, asking something like "Why can't I get my smart phone to access the corporate wi-fi?" or "How can I get my personal laptop to connect to the office Internet?" is likely to be less suspicious than asking "How do I configure Tor to get through the corporate firewall?"

2.3.3 Sharing

There are four options for using Tor and/or sharing your resources with others on the Tor network:

- Run as a client only.
- Bridge relay.

- Nonexit relay (transit relay).
- Exit relay.

Most users stay with the default of running Tor as a client only. This is safest and simplest, and should be the least conspicuous option as well. If you know what you are doing and have spare network bandwidth, you may want to configure your system as a Tor bridge or a Tor relay.

Running a bridge relay is the first level, and can be considered the safest way of sharing resources on the Tor network. Bridges are safe, because running as a Tor bridge your system will not forward any Tor traffic to the Internet—which means a bridge operator's IP address will never appear in a server log. Also, because bridges are not listed publicly anywhere, your system's IP address won't be easily identified by attackers.

The next level of sharing is to run as a transit relay. In this case, your system sends and receives only encrypted Tor network traffic between other Tor clients: a transit relay can act as the entry relay (accepting encrypted network traffic from a Tor client), or it can accept/forward data between another transit relay and an exit relay.

Acting as a transit relay, there is minimal risk of being connected to specific (forbidden or illegal) content. However, your ISP may have terms of use that forbid participating, or they may simply prefer that you not use bandwidth for this type of application.

Running as an exit node is the next level, and comes with somewhat greater risk because your system may be handling unencrypted data (e. g., if the end user is accessing a web server that does not support HTTPS; see sidebar in Chapter 1, "HTTP Secure and HTTPS Everywhere"). If that data is being monitored for forbidden content, you may risk being held (incorrectly) as responsible for that content.

The Tor network depends on users around the world who share their resources. If you want to share resources but are not confident in your technical ability, you can also donate cash to Tor exit node providers (see "Support the Tor Network: Donate to Exit Node Providers," at https://blog.torproject.org/blog/support-tor-network-donate-exit-node-providers, for more information).

Configuring a Tor relay (see https://www.torproject.org/docs/tor-doc-relay.html.en) is not terribly complicated for those with modest system administration skills, and comfortable with handling their own operational security (see https://trac.torproject.org/projects/tor/wiki/doc/OperationalSecurity). See also Chapter 5 for more about sharing resources on the Tor network.

2.3.4 Services

This panel is for adding and configuring Tor hidden services. At this writing, Vidalia hidden services support is still relatively new, and Tor documentation warns that it may still have bugs in it.

Vidalia hidden service configuration is easier to use than setting things up manually, but it also lacks some of the more advanced features available only when administering a hidden service through torrc, the Tor configuration file.

For more information about setting up and using hidden services, see Chapter 6.

2.3.5 Appearances

This panel allows you to change the language used by the Vidalia interface as well as choose different GUI styles. You can also choose to display or hide Tor-related icons on your desktop.

2.3.6 Advanced

Three general sections in this panel includes the following:

Tor control. Setting up how Tor networking software connects to the Tor network through the local host, also setting up authentication to use Tor through the system.

Tor configuration file. Where the Tor configuration file (torrc) is located, and an option to edit the currently loaded version of the configuration file. The file can be edited and applied to the current session only, or saved for future use.

Tor data directory. The directory where Tor stores necessary data, such as cached versions of the Tor consensus directory (the list of all Tor relays distributed by Tor directory servers) and cryptographic keys required to communicate on the Tor network.

2.4 USING TOR BROWSER

The Tor Browser is a modified version of the Firefox ESR. Iceweasel, the browser included with the Tails distribution, is also based on the Mozilla browser project. Both Tor browsers are functionally identical (or nearly so), and should be familiar to anyone who has used Firefox (or related browsers).

Users should be extremely cautious about changing Tor browser settings, as the defaults have been chosen carefully by Tor Project developers for maximum safety and usefulness. Changing some settings may cause obvious problems for maintaining anonymity, such as allowing the browser to remember browser history or disabling warnings when sites try to install add-ons. Other changes may cause problems that are not so obvious, so in general, it is probably best to leave the browser settings alone.

2.5 WHEN TOR WON'T CONNECT

Tor will not always work the first time without additional configuration. Here are some general guidelines for troubleshooting software that can be tried when Tor doesn't work for you, and some other things to check that are specific to Tor.

2.5.1 Basic Troubleshooting

The first thing to check when troubleshooting a network problem is whether the system is connected to the network. Before starting Tor, you should verify that the Internet connection is working, that all cables (if needed) are connected.

Often, removing all plugs and blowing on them, then replacing them, will solve the problem.

Another trick that solves many problems is to turn the system off and then on again.

2.5.2 Do You Need a Proxy?

You may be able to check your browser's or system's network configuration to see if a proxy is required to access the Internet. View your browser settings by choosing Preferences from the browser pulldown menu (proxy settings are usually shown under an "Advanced" settings tab or panel).

Your browser may be set to use your system's proxy configuration, in which case you should open the relevant system configuration tool (some browsers will open your system network configuration tool for you). If there is a proxy, it should be listed in the configuration display.

To configure Tor to use the proxy, use Vidalia's Settings shortcut and go to the Network panel. Click on the checkbox that says "I use a proxy to access the Internet," and you will be prompted to enter proxy information (you may be able to get at least some of this information from your system configuration, as noted above).

2.5.3 Checking the Tor Log

Open the Tor log, advanced view, and you may see messages that give an indication of what is not working. For example, if your system clock is not set properly, Tor cannot work (your computer is masquerading with an IP address that is usually connected to computers in another country, so Tor needs to reconcile the time between what a remote server thinks it is and what your system knows to be the local time).

While some of the messages in the Tor log will be unhelpful, try to read through them anyway, as they often indicate (if a bit cryptically) what the problem is. For example, you may see a message about a program being missing—in that case, the solution is to reinstall Tor. If a message says something about an address already being in use (or being unreachable), you may need to restart the system or reconfigure Tor for use with a restrictive firewall.

2.5.4 Reconfiguring Tor for Firewalls

If you are behind a restrictive firewall (that is, one that only allows access to web servers), you can reconfigure Tor to avoid using forbidden *ports*.

A port is like an address on a computer for a particular program. Internet protocols send network data to and from a particular program running on an Internet server by specifying the server's IP address along with the port number of the program.

A restrictive firewall would limit traffic to data being sent to web servers on ports 80 (for unencrypted HTTP) and 443 (for encrypted HTTPS).

To use Tor behind a firewall that filters on port numbers this strictly, use Vidalia's Settings shortcut and go to the Network panel. Click on the checkbox that says "My firewall only lets me connect to certain ports," and you will be prompted to enter valid ports (the default is to allow only ports 80 and 443, the "well known" ports for the HTTP web protocol).

If antivirus software is blocking your access to Tor, you can either try using Tails (which will boot without starting any software installed on your system's fixed drives), or disable/uninstall the antivirus program.

2.5.5 If Tor Still Won't Connect

If Tor is still not connecting, your ISP may be blocking Tor explicitly by filtering on Tor relay addresses and preventing you from accessing any Tor transit relays. Some countries actively block Tor, but so may individual ISPs or any organization that runs its own firewall. This is where Tor bridges are useful, because they are not listed in any complete and publicly accessible way.

Setting up to use Tor with a bridge is relatively simple: first, find the addresses for some bridges, and then configure network settings in Vidalia to use the bridges by checking the box labeled "My ISP blocks connections to the Tor network." You will be able to enter bridge addresses in the panel that appears.

Adding a single bridge may be enough, but configuring more than one bridge is preferred. If one bridge becomes unavailable, having one or more other bridges configured means your Tor connection is less likely to be terminated prematurely.

For more detailed information on how to find and use Tor bridges, see Chapter 4.

CHAPTER 3

Using Tails

Tails (see https://tails.boum.org/) is a customized and stripped-down Linux distribution that includes Tor as well as other features to provide an operating system that enhances privacy. Tails is a subproject of Tor Project. Tails is sometimes incorrectly referred to as "TAILS", from the acronym "The Amnesic Incognito Live System."

Although there are other Linux distributions whose design goal is anonymity, many users prefer Tails because of its affiliation with the Tor Project. Tails implementers work with Tor Project developers to reduce vulnerabilities and to improve overall security.

As a Linux distribution, Tails includes a number of applications and features that are not readily available to those using Tor Browser Bundle in Windows or OS X. Because Tails is the running operating system, things that would cause loss of anonymity on an ordinary Windows or OS X system are not problems.

●●●───

More About Tor

Tails on Apple Computers
Although it is reported to be possible to boot Tails on an Apple computer, it can be far from trivial. In fact, it can be quite a mess and (currently) should be avoided if you have another reasonable option (e.g., using Tails from any "wintel" system or using Tor Browser Bundle on OS X).

If you must boot Tails on a Macintosh, check the Tails forum (see https://tails.boum.org/forum) for recent threads about using Tails on a system that runs OS X.

───

For example, your operating system can reveal your IP address when opening a file that contains web content. When you download a file through the Tor network, you do so anonymously: the operators of the server that you downloaded from will only be able to associate that download with the Tor exit node you used.

However, if you open that file and it contains a URL, your word processor will attempt to download that content: and now the people who run the server can connect your copy of the downloaded file with your real IP address.

It does not matter whether the creator of the file put in the downloadable files as a strategy to identify the downloader, or as an innocent way to deliver content: the resulting Internet connection to download that content reveals your identity.

Opening an application file in a program that is not explicitly reconfigured (and, possibly, modified) to be using Tor means that the program will use the public Internet, with all that means: the user's content will be exposed on the local network and the user's IP address will be accessible to the remote server or anyone with sufficient access to that system (instead of being protected in a Tor circuit).

With Tails, the network stack has been modified so that all Internet connectivity is routed by default through the Tor network. If the Tor network is not accessible, then the public Internet is not accessible, either.

When using Tor Browser Bundle on a Windows, OS X, or other (ordinary) Linux distribution, your system may inadvertently give you away when you open files that contain web content, because on those system only the Tor Browser Bundle applications (basically, just the Tor Browser) use Tor, while other active public Internet connections can happen at the same time as the Tor session.

That is not to say that Tails can't handle non-Tor network traffic— it just is configured to use the public Internet protocols only for connecting to remote servers through Tor relays.

Also, there are times when it is necessary to use an "unsafe" browser to access a service, for example, with networks that require a login or registration to activate the connection. That is why the *Unsafe Browser* is included as an option in Tails.

3.1 WHAT IS IN TAILS

Tails includes enough software to do most typical desktop computing tasks (e.g., e-mail, web, document creation/editing for all major applications, as well as full networking capabilities and standard operating system functions available to any Linux system). Tails bundled software (see https://tails.boum.org/doc/about/features/index.en.html for a complete list) should be familiar to anyone who has used Linux; key software packages to note are as follows:

- *Firefox/Iceweasel*: Iceweasel (see http://wiki.debian.org/Iceweasel) is a fork (modified version) of Firefox that incorporates some security features and is free of trademarked artwork owned by Mozilla, the organization that publishes Firefox (it's a long story, mostly about licensing issues; for some idea of the origins of the problem, see "Debian bug report on use of Mozilla Firefox trademark without permission" at http://bugs.debian.org/cgi-bin/bugreport.cgi?bug = 354622, and "mozilla thunderbird trademark restrictions/still dfsg free?" at http://lists.debian.org/debian-legal/2004/12/msg00328.html).
- *Pidgin/OTR*: Pidgin (see http://www.pidgin.im) is an instant messaging client; OTR (Off-the-Record Messaging, see http://www.cypherpunks.ca/otr/index.php) is a plugin that enables private instant messaging. The two programs are preinstalled/configured in Tails.
- *Gnu Privacy Guard*: Also known as GnuPG (see http://gnupg.org), Gnu Privacy Guard is a *de facto* standard for doing public key cryptography (data encryption and decryption and digital signatures). Tails also includes GnuPG plugins so that data can be encrypted within application programs such as the gedit text editor (see http://projects.gnome.org/gedit) and the OpenOffice.org office productivity suite (see http://openoffice.org).
- *OpenOffice.org*: An adequate (for many) office productivity suite; encryption is not currently integrated, so for encrypting, decrypting, digitally signing, or verifying digital signatures in text documents, gedit is preferred as it does include GnuPG support.
- *Metadata Anonymization Toolkit (MAT)* (https://mat.boum.org): A GUI toolbox that can be used to strip out metadata from word processing, graphics, media, or other types of data files. Metadata includes information about the user and the system creating the files, and can reveal identifying information about the editor or creator of the file. If you send or receive data files and wish to protect your anonymity, consider using this toolkit.
- *Unsafe Web Browser*: This is another version of Iceweasel, which is a version of Firefox Mozilla ESR. And this version is configured to allow unsafe web browsing (as when required to activate a web

connection). The home page has a lot of red warnings, along with an explanation of how and why to use the Unsafe Web Browser.

These are only some of the featured applications that are accessed easily through the Tails GUI. Other programs accessible through the Tails menus include:

- GIMP (bitmap graphics);
- Inkscape (vector-based drawing);
- Scribus (desktop publishing);
- Audacity (for recording, editing, and playing audio).

This is far from a comprehensive list of included software. As a Linux distribution, Tails includes numerous command-line utilities, as well as an assortment of other applications. You can use the desktop to explore the programs that have been included (under the Applications menu, accessed from the upper left corner of the desktop).

You may also use the Synaptic (http://www.nongnu.org/synaptic/) package (software installation) manager tool for managing installed software, if you booted with an administrative password to allow modification to system settings. You can use Synaptic to see what packages are installed, but not to install packages that were not included with the Tails distribution (see below for more about installing extra software under Tails).

3.2 SETTING UP FOR TAILS

Much of the beauty of using Tails resides in booting it from any (almost) computer from a USB thumb drive or DVD, without leaving any "evidence" on the computer being used. Tails does not have to be "installed" on the system, nor does it save any kind of logs, cookies, or any other evidence on the system drive.

To do this, the system running Tails needs to be able to boot from a DVD or USB drive, which (as noted) means that it is usually easiest to get running from a computer designed to run Windows (or Linux) than from a modern Apple computer.

3.2.1 Getting Tails

The first step to using it is to download the Tails DVD image (ISO) (from https://tails.boum.org/download/index.en.html) and burning it to a DVD; rather than attempting to document from scratch how to do this, the Tails website links to Ubuntu's instructions for burning an ISO (see https://help.ubuntu.com/community/BurningIsoHowto). Once you have a bootable DVD, you are ready to run Tails by putting the DVD into the system disc drive and then rebooting the system.

The Tails ISO download will be about 850 Mb of data, so on a broadband connection it should take a few minutes to complete. Be sure to also download the Tails ISO digital signature; once both are downloaded, verify the signature before continuing. See Appendix A for detailed instructions on verifying digital signatures for Tails.

3.2.2 Configuring the System to Boot Tails

Most computers are configured to boot from whatever operating system is installed on the hard drive. You can install other operating systems, and then choose which to boot when powering the computer up, but with Tails you will want to reconfigure the system hardware to boot from an attached device (USB drive) or from the disc drive if there is a bootable DVD inserted.

On most systems, you can change the "boot order" of the computer by accessing its BIOS configuration utility. This process can vary widely from system to system, but the basic process is this:

- Turn the computer off and then on again, carefully watching the screen for messages like "Press ESC to enter SETUP" or "PRESS ALT-F12 to configure BIOS."
- Press the key indicated to access the BIOS configuration tool. This program is almost always displayed in simple text and uses the arrow keys, ESC, Enter, and some function keys to select and change configuration items.
- Change the configuration to allow the system to boot from operating systems on removable media (DVD/CD disc drive, or USB attached). The simplest way to do this is browsing through all the configuration options. The option may be called something like "boot order" or it may be offered under an "advanced" option.

As there are so many different types of computer hardware, and because products change over time, it can be worthwhile to search online for more details about your particular system (if you are having trouble getting it configured). Ubuntu often has particularly helpful resources for setting up a system to boot from a LiveCD Linux distribution, for example, see the article "BIOS is not set to boot from CD or DVD drive" at https://help.ubuntu.com/community/ BootFromCD#BIOS_is_not_set_to_boot_from_CD_or_DVD_drive on the Ubuntu website.

3.3 USING TAILS

Tails can be booted either from a disc or from removable USB drive; there are advantages and disadvantages to each:

Using Tails from a DVD means:

- Greater confidence that no traces will be left of any Tails sessions. That is, nothing should be written on disc storage of the system running Tails, and nothing will be written to the Tails disc itself.
- Greater confidence that your copy of Tails will not be modified by an attacker. Burning the Tails distribution on a DVD-R (read-only DVD) means that no one can add, remove, or modify the Tails distribution software.
- Every time a new version of Tails is released, you must download and burn a new DVD (and get rid of outdated versions of Tails).
- You need to carry (and keep secure) a bootable DVD. Appropriate precautions should be taken, especially if traveling to unfriendly regions: labeling the DVD "Tails: anonymous Internet" or the like may not be prudent.

Using Tails from a USB drive means:

- As a writeable medium, if the USB device is large enough you can configure a persistent volume (a section of the device on which you can store data, software, and configuration files). The Tails persistent volume is encrypted and passphrase-protected, so you can use it to safely store personal files and working documents, extra software you need to work with in Tails, custom configurations of your Tails system and application tools, and encryption keys.
- As a writeable medium, an attacker with physical access to the thumb drive could maliciously modify or remove key software, or introduce malware (virus or keylogging software), compromising your security.

- Tails installed to an SD data card or small USB drive is very portable and can be carried inconspicuously.
- Upgrading Tails on a USB drive is simple, even with persistent storage enabled, and the drive can be reused (unlike DVDs). However, it is recommended that you upgrade USB drives from a running version of the newest released Tails, which implies burning it to DVD in any case (not mandatory, but easier and recommended).
- Not all computers can be booted from USB devices.

The decision to run Tails from DVD or USB drive will depend on the specific factors relating to how, where, and by whom Tails will be used.

3.3.1 Booting Tails

If booting from DVD, insert the DVD into the system disc drive and power cycle the computer. If the system NetBIOS has been configured correctly to allow booting from DVD, and if the DVD has been properly burned, the system should boot to splash screen with the option of booting "Live" or "Live (failsafe)." Choose "Live" with the up or down arrow keys, and then press Enter.

If Tails doesn't boot at this point, try again, but choose "Live (failsafe)." It boots Tails but disables some features (those known to cause problems on booting).

If Tails "Live" boots correctly, you should next see a dialog box (or two) prompting for "More options?" and for "User persistence?" (only when a persistent volume is detected on the Live Boot device).

More options include:

- Set an administrative password, to allow superuser access to the operating system. If the password isn't set, you won't be able to do any "system" functions. This includes things like reviewing log files; in general, you won't need to do any system administration, but reviewing the logs can be helpful when troubleshooting system and network problems. This is also required to access any system discs on the computer booted from DVD/USB drive.
- A *camouflage* option, booting Tails with a GUI setup that looks (at least superficially) like a Windows XP desktop. Some users may find it useful for "blending in" while using Tails in public.

If there is a persistent volume on the thumb drive, Tails gives you the option of using it during your session. As already noted, persistence should be used sparingly and only when necessary.

3.3.2 Shutting Tails Down

Some users may find it necessary to power down their Tails sessions as quickly as possible. If an attacker gains access to your system while it is running Tails, they can extract from working memory a great deal of information about you and your network activity. This defeats the purpose of being anonymous, and can be catastrophic if you use persistent storage for keys or other secrets.

Thus, one of the design goals for Tails was to make it possible to shut the system down as quickly and easily as possible.

You can shut down (power off) or reboot the system from the System/Administration menu (at the top and near the upper left corner). Once you "pull the trigger" to shut down, the system clears out memory and halts itself immediately.

Another, faster, way to power down/reboot is by clicking on the red system power button in the upper right corner of the display. The two choices are "Shut down immediately" and "Reboot immediately"; click one or the other and the action follows immediately.

The fastest way to shut down Tails is to remove the Tails Live boot medium. Physically remove the Tails boot DVD, or (even better) remove the thumb drive or SD card. If the boot medium is removed, all system activity is halted and the system shuts down.

3.3.3 Installing Tails on a USB Drive

The Tails system includes a program called Tails LiveUSB Creator, which enables the process of creating a bootable USB drive. At this writing, USB devices can be made bootable only with an extra program, like LiveUSB Creator.

If you cannot run the version of LiveUSB Creator included with Tails (that is, if you cannot burn your own copy of the Tails DVD and boot your system to Tails from that DVD), you can run some other program that does the same thing as LiveUSB Creator (see Section 3.3.4).

This process works on SD cards (including mini- and micro-SD cards) as well as USB storage devices.

The recommended way to get Tails on a bootable USB drive is to use the Tails LiveUSB Creator program. Boot the system to Tails, and click on "Applications" in the upper left corner of the screen. Scroll down to "Tails" for access to tools for using Tails.

Choose "Tails USB installer" to open Tails LiveUSB Creator and begin. Upon starting, the Tails LiveUSB Creator opens a dialog box with three large buttons:

- *Clone & Install*: to copy the currently running version of Tails onto a USB device, overwriting any data on that device.
- *Clone & Upgrade*: to copy the currently running version of Tails onto a USB device that has an older version of Tails already installed on it. This overwrites only the Tails installation; other partitions on the device are not affected.
- *Upgrade from ISO*: to upgrade a USB device currently running an older version of Tails, from an ISO file containing a more recent version.

The safest way to go is to boot the system using the latest version of Tails on a DVD. Then, when you "clone" the currently running version of Tails, you are using the most up-to-date version.

Choosing to Clone & Install will (should) wipe clean the USB device and install the currently running version of Tails onto it. Doing so means that any malware hidden on the USB device's filesystem should be eliminated—but it also means that any data stored by the user will also be eliminated.

When there is data already on the thumb drive, you can use the Copy & Upgrade option. This way, any persistent volumes you've configured on the drive will be left alone and only the volume containing the older Tails software will be wiped and rewritten with updated software.

Finally, if you are unable to burn Tails to DVD and boot from that disc—but you do have a copy of Tails installed on a USB device, you can download the current Tails ISO, boot from whatever version of Tails you've got, and use the last choice, "Upgrade from ISO."

The problem with the last option is that it has some risks. For example, you should try to avoid connecting to any network while using the outdated version of Tails—if it has a security vulnerability, you would be at risk of exposing yourself by using it online.

Also, you should be especially careful about verifying the downloaded ISO's digital signature, because you are installing it "sight unseen" on USB. The other methods require that the current version of Tails boot on the system, so you can use Tor to check that your version of Tails is, indeed, current and running correctly.

3.3.4 Installing Tails to a USB Device, Manually

It is possible to install Tails "by hand" onto a USB/SD device (see "Manually Installing onto a USB Stick" at https://tails.boum.org/doc/first_steps/manual_usb_installation/index.en.html), but doing so requires downloading and using a program that does the same thing that the Tails Linux LiveUSB Creator program does.

HOWEVER, this method does not support setting up a persistent volume for storing data on the USB device.

At this writing, there are different programs recommended for Windows, Mac OS X, and Linux systems. The programs currently recommended are:

- *Windows*: Pendrivelinux (see http://www.pendrivelinux.com) publishes a utility called Universal USB Installer (see http://www.pendrivelinux.com/universal-usb-installer-easy-as-1-2-3), that will write a Live-bootable Linux distribution to a USB device.
- *Mac OS X*: rEFInd (http://sourceforge.net/projects/refind), an Extensible Firmware Interface (EFI) boot manager, is currently recommended.
- *Linux*: a utility called `isohybrid` is included with popular Linux distributions, including Ubuntu and Debian.

Up-to-date instructions for using all of these programs are available at the Tor Project website. And be sure to check that website for the latest on which LiveUSB creator software is recommended for your platform of choice.

3.3.5 Upgrading Tails ("Clone & Upgrade")

Tails installed on a writeable USB device can be upgraded using the Tails USB Installer (see Section 3.3.3) by choosing the Clone & Upgrade option.

Because the installer uses the version of Tails that is currently running, you'll need to download and install the latest version of Tails, burn it to DVD and boot from that DVD before starting the USB installer. Clone & Upgrade will update the USB device and will leave any persistent data storage partitions intact.

Most important to remember: do not boot from the USB device you want to upgrade; boot from the latest version of Tails on a DVD, and use the installer only after you've plugged in the USB device. I find it easiest to remember if I remove the USB drive to be updated from the system before trying to boot to the latest version of Tails.

3.3.6 Persistent Storage on Tails

Tails supports the use of persistent storage when booting from a writeable medium, such as USB device. An encrypted partition can be created, and configured Tails to allow storage of data or application files, configuration files, specific directories, web history files, and more.

Before using persistence on Tails, you should educate yourself about the potential dangers of using persistence. Start with the article "Warnings About Persistence" (on the Tails website at https://tails.boum.org/doc/first_steps/persistence/warnings/index.en.html),   which lists and explains some of the issues that can cause problems for users trying to retain anonymity with Tails.

These issues include:

- *If you lose possession of a Tails boot drive with persistent memory*, an attacker can open it and see that it contains Tails plus an encrypted volume. The fact that there are secrets on your USB drive means an attacker can use a variety of tactics to extract your passphrase.
- *If you use persistent storage*, you are able to modify system and application configurations. This may make Tails more convenient to use, for example, to simplify network configuration, or for running Tails with a proxy—however, it can also lead to problems. A changed configuration file can inadvertently allow information to leak, or it can reduce anonymity by presenting a unique system profile (see Panopticlick, at https://panopticlick.eff.org).

With data persistence you can even inadvertently save configuration files you didn't intend to by linking files from a directory into the home folder, or by setting a custom directory to be made persistent (for more, see Section 3.3.7).

- *With persistence, it is possible to install additional software to use with Tails.* The latest version (0.18) even includes an experimental feature that will automatically install additional software of your choice—and will also automatically install any upgrades once a network connection has been established (Tails offers a brief explanation of how to use this feature on this page: https://tails.boum.org/doc/first_steps/persistence/configure/index.en.html#additional_packages).

This "live" installation uses your list to install software on your Tails USB drive, as long as it is installable with the Debian Linux APT installer utility. This is a great power, as it allows you to create your own personal toolkit to use with Tails—but also a great responsibility.

Even the most benign software sometimes harbors honest bugs (or malware) that reduces or breaks user anonymity. If you must use a particular program that is not included with Tails, consider using it only when your system is not connected to the Internet. For software that requires a network connection, consider contacting the Tails or Tor projects for advice.

- *Using data persistence to install unapproved plugins or to reconfigure the browser plugins included with Tails can also reduce your anonymity or even expose you completely*—for the same reasons that you are warned against installing browser plugins with Tails.
- *Be careful with data persistence.* Use it sparingly, only as and when needed. Also, use the configuration wizard to turn persistence on only for items that must be persistent, and avoid doing anything to change configurations from Tails defaults unless absolutely necessary (and unless you know what you are doing).
- *Access persistent storage only when needed.* Even if you've installed a persistent data partition on your Tails USB device, you can choose not to access it when booting Tails. If you don't access it, the partition is not mounted—and the passphrase to access the data is not entered. This can help you to use Tor more safely in environments where you may be under digital (keylogging) or visual surveillance.

3.3.7 Configuring Persistence

Access the persistence wizard through the Applications/Tails or Applications/System Tools menus ("Configure persistent volume").

If you are going to use it, the Tails page on Persistence (https://tails.boum.org/doc/first_steps/persistence/index.en.html) is a good place to start, with links to warnings on using persistence as well as instructions for:

- Create and configure the persistent volume (see https://tails.boum.org/doc/first_steps/persistence/configure/index.en.htm). Basically, the menu option "Applications ▶ Tails ▶ Configure persistent storage," and follow the prompts and read the instructions. "Persistent Volume Features" (https://tails.boum.org/doc/first_steps/persistence/configure/index.en.html#index3h1) explains all the options for types of data and configuration files that can be stored.
- Enable and use the persistent volume (see https://tails.boum.org/doc/first_steps/persistence/use/index.en.html). Basically, you enable persistence when logging in (there's a checkbox); if you enable it you'll have to enter the passphrase. You can also make the access read-only, so no changes can be written to the media. Once booted, you can access files in a folder named "Persistent" in the Home folder.
- Delete the persistent volume (see https://tails.boum.org/doc/first_steps/persistence/delete/index.en.html). Basically, the menu option "Applications ▶ Tails ▶ Delete persistent storage," and click on the Delete button. Then, create an encrypted partition (see https://tails.boum.org/doc/encryption_and_privacy/encrypted_volumes/index.en.html) to wipe the drive, which also deletes the old partitions used for booting Tails and for persistent storage. Next, you want to securely clean available disc space (see https://tails.boum.org/doc/encryption_and_privacy/secure_deletion/index.en.html#clean_disk_space) and then reinstall Tails (see https://tails.boum.org/doc/first_steps/usb_installation/index.en.html), restart from that device, and, finally, create a new persistent volume (see https://tails.boum.org/doc/first_steps/persistence/configure/index.en.html).

3.3.8 Whisperback

Perhaps more than for most software projects, Tails (and the Tor Project) depends on accurate and up-to-date information about any bugs that might be found in the code. Because they are used to secure personal safety/freedom, every user has a vested interest in reporting bugs and having them resolved as quickly as possible.

To simplify bug reporting—as well as make it safe—the Tails Project developed the Whisperback program. As described in Report a bug (see https://tails.boum.org/doc/first_steps/bug_reporting), to start Whisperback, pull down the menu option Applications/System Tools/ Whisperback (from the upper left corner of the display).

3.3.9 KeePassX

From its project page, KeePassX (http://www.keepassx.org) "is an OpenSource password safe which helps you to manage your passwords in an easy and secure way. It uses a highly encrypted database locked with one master key."

Features include a secure (passphrase-protected) and searchable database for user passphrases, a strong passphrase generator, and is published as Free Software under the GNU General Public License.

If you use data persistence to store login credentials, you should store them securely by using KeePassX as provided.

From the Tails website, see "Manage passwords with KeePassX" (https://tails.boum.org/doc/encryption_and_privacy/manage_passwords/ index.en.html) for instructions as well as a summary of some of the benefits of using it:

- KeePassX lets you store passwords in an encrypted database, protected by a single passphrase.
- Access all password-protected services securely, but remember only one passphrase.
- KeePassX generates strong passphrases, without any need to make them easy to remember. Users get the benefit of the strongest possible passphrases, without the difficulty of trying to remember them.

3.3.10 Metadata Anonymization Toolkit

When an application file—a word processing document, a photograph, an audio recording, etc.—is created, the program that creates it often includes *metadata*: data that is about the data in the file. So, for example, you might open a Word document and find the name, phone number, and e-mail address of the person on whose computer the document was written. For obvious reasons, if you are trying to remain anonymous you will not want your data files to reveal your identity.

The Metadata Anonymization Toolkit (MAT) is a toolkit for stripping metadata out of application files including:

- Portable Network Graphics (.png)
- JPEG (.jpg, .jpeg, ...)
- Open Documents (.odt, .odx, .ods, ...)
- Office OpenXml (.docx, .pptx, .xlsx, ...)
- Portable Document Fileformat (.pdf)
- Tape ARchives (.tar, .tar.bz2, .tar.gz, ...)
- Zip (.zip)
- MPEG Audio (.mp3, .mp2, .mp1, ...)
- Ogg Vorbis (.ogg, ...)
- Free Lossless Audio Codec (.flac)
- Torrent (.torrent).

MAT is an official part of the Tails project, home page at https://mat.boum.org/.

Using MAT in the Tails desktop as a GUI application is simple, as long as you accept the default behavior when it cleans a file, which is for MAT to make a copy of the file being cleaned, and name it `filename.cleaned.jpg` (or with any other valid file extension). So the original file, with metadata, is still there—but now there is a "cleaned" copy of it.

MAT can also be run from the command line, where you can see available options by starting the program like this:

```
$ mat -d filename.ext
```

That command will return (to the display) the metadata stored in a file. To clean a file and save a backup copy (the default behavior for the GUI application), you would enter the command like this:

```
$ mat -b filename.ext
```

Entering the command "mat" with no options will return a help screen with a handful of other options.

3.3.11 Claws Mail
Claws Mail (http://www.claws-mail.org) is an open source e-mail client, included with Tails to provide a way to access an e-mail account anonymously.

You do not want to use Claws in Tails over Tor to get your personal e-mail. That would associate your personal e-mail account with the Tor session. Claws is useful for accessing an anonymously setup e-mail account, one that you access only via the Tor network.

If you have such an account setup, you will need e-mail configuration settings (inbound/outbound mail servers, authentication requirements, etc.). And if you want to use that account regularly, you might consider enabling persistence to store Claws Mail profiles and locally stored e-mail, with the Tails Persistence wizard (see Section 3.3.7).

Users not comfortable with several panels of configuration to set up e-mail may prefer to create an account on a webmail site. However, keep in mind that when accessing webmail through Tor, the webmail service may detect logins to your account from IP addresses spread all over the world, which may trigger some sort of response.

3.3.12 GNU Privacy Guard

GNU Privacy Guard (GnuPG; see https://www.gnupg.org) is the *de facto* standard for open source encryption and cryptography. See also, "Simple Steps to Data Encryption" (Loshin) for more about how to use GnuPG.

GnuPG is installed in Tails, but there is no GnuPG application accessible from the GUI desktop.

You can encrypt or sign a file, validate a signed file or decrypt an OpenPGP-standard file, with a right-click on an item displayed in the file browser.

In the gedit text processor (Applications/Accessories) you can also encrypt, decrypt, sign, and verify text, just by highlighting the text to be processed, and selecting the option desired.

If you will be using GnuPG with Tails on a regular basis, you will likely have your own keys (that can in no way be connected with your real identity) plus the keys of people with whom you correspond, on a GnuPG keyring. Storing this keyring in the Tails persistent volume can be very convenient.

Using GnuPG at the command line is often simpler. See Appendix A for examples of using GnuPG to verify the signatures on Tails and Tor Project downloads.

CHAPTER 4

Tor Relays, Bridges, and Obfsproxy

This chapter is about how to use Tor effectively even when a powerful adversary—such as a government—is actively filtering all Tor network traffic. While many users will have no problem using Tor to easily and quickly connect to any Internet service, in some countries it is not enough.

Depending on how important it is to the adversary to filter all objectionable content, some adversaries may forbid use of any censorship circumvention tools like Tor. In some cases, if the firewalls detect Tor network activity, those sessions are blocked.

This chapter discusses how such national-level filtering can be (and is) done.

There is a great deal of academic research related to online anonymity and anonymous network protocols, which means that there are a lot of very clever people working on finding ways to defeat Tor—both in the free world and in closed-off societies. What's more, much of the academic work is published freely and available to those working to defeat online anonymity.

What this means is that when one hole in the protocol is fixed, adversaries will attempt to discover other flaws that may allow them to defeat censorship circumvention. It is an ongoing "arms race" between Tor Project and those aiming to filter Tor traffic; with each victory, the other side must find a work-around.

4.1 WHEN BASIC TOR IS NOT ENOUGH

When I use the term "adversary," I generally refer to an organizational or political entity, organization, group, or individual who has the resources to monitor all your network activity in order to prevent you from communicating freely or to punish you for forbidden activity—and the will to do so.

When a government decides that all Internet access must be filtered, they may also decide that using any censorship circumvention tools, such as Tor, must also be blocked.

One well-documented instance of a country filtering Tor is described in the paper, "How China Is Blocking Tor" (http://arxiv.org/abs/1204.0447). Written in 2012, the paper describes how the Great Firewall of China (GFC) actively blocked Tor traffic based on research done in December 2011. (See also the MIT Technology Review article, "How China Blocks the Tor Anonymity Network" at http://www.technologyreview.com/view/427413/how-china-blocks-the-tor-anonymity-network.) Although the paper describes how China was able to block Tor traffic in 2011, since then, Tor has continued to adapt to the attack while the people who run the GFC have also been adapting.

4.1.1 How China Blocked Tor

The paper, written by Philipp Winter and Stefan Lindskog of Karlstad University, describes how they discovered that the GFC was filtering Tor traffic with the end result that it could terminate any successful Tor connection from inside China within 15 minutes, and could block all public Tor relay nodes.

The GFC blocks access in three ways, by filtering:

- the *Tor Project website*. Attempts to connect to the Tor Project website at torproject.org were filtered. Blocking the website makes it more difficult for users in China to even get the Tor software necessary to initiate anonymous web sessions.
- the *Tor public network*. There are nine Tor directory authorities, servers that distribute information about active Tor relays. The researchers discovered that the GFC blocked all access to those servers inside China. The GFC could also block almost all of the Tor relays described in the Tor directory consensus.
- the *Tor protocol*. In order to circumvent filtering on public Tor relay nodes, Tor developers came up with the idea of using "bridge relays." These are Tor relays that are *not* published publicly; the idea being that that makes it harder for an adversary (e.g., China) to discover them and filter them. Unfortunately, the Chinese were able to discover ways to identify network traffic that uses the Tor protocol; the intended destination for such traffic is assumed to be a

Tor relay and the IP for that destination is added to the GFC filters.

The rest of this chapter explains the solutions implemented to work around the GFC, specifically, Tor *bridge relays* (see https://www. torproject.org/docs/bridges.html.en) and *obfsproxy* ("obfuscated proxy," see https://www.torproject.org/projects/obfsproxy.html.en).

A bridge relay is like any other Tor transit relay, only it is not publicly listed and it is generally used only for entering the Tor network from places where public Tor relays are blocked. Tor Project is experimenting with different mechanisms for distributing bridge relays to Tor users in ways that are more difficult for nation-state adversaries to detect.

Obfsproxy ("obfuscating proxy") obscures the headers on the network packets so that they do not look like Tor packets, but rather the packets are made to appear as if they are "regular" Internet (web) traffic. Obfsproxy incorporates two important concepts:

- *Obfuscated bridge*: an intermediary system which accepts obfuscated Tor network traffic and forwards it onward, bypassing filtering for Tor by protocol content.
- *Pluggable transport*: a special plugin program that accepts as input a stream of raw Tor network traffic and returns as output a stream of network traffic that appears to be some other protocol. There are currently a number of planned (and a smaller number of deployed) transports already in development (see "Tor: Pluggable Transports" at https://www.torproject.org/docs/pluggable-transports. html.en).

4.1.2 Is Tor Down, or Do You Need a Bridge

As with any software, when things go wrong with connecting to Tor, it means one of three things:

- You're doing it wrong.
- Something is broken.
- Someone is blocking Tor.

You're doing it wrong: One of the design goals of the Tor Project is to make it as usable and accessible for regular users as possible. So if

Tor is not working correctly, you should know it when the Tor Browser starts up the Tor check page, at https://check.torproject.org. If there are no obvious problems, such as connecting from inside a region where Tor is actively being blocked or from behind an organizational firewall, it is worth going through some troubleshooting first (starting by rebooting your system after verifying that you have installed a validated version of the software). See "How to Troubleshoot Common Problems in Tor" (https://securityinabox.org/en/tor_troubleshooting) for some suggestions on troubleshooting.

Assuming, however, that you've double-checked everything, that you have configured Tor to use the appropriate ports and proxy servers, and that you don't have any other software (for example, virus checking programs) that might be blocking you from using Tor, the next possibility to consider is the second point.

Something is broken: Tor software, like any software, can have bugs in it. Updates to the TBB are released relatively often, both for new features and for bug fixes. If you think you have a bug, you can check the Tor wiki/bug tracker to see if someone else has already reported the bug—or to report the bug yourself (https://trac.torproject.org/projects/tor). You may also wish to check the Tor Project mailing list to see if this is an active issue, and if so, what to do about it (see Appendix C for more information about where to look).

If it's not a bug, and you're doing everything correctly, you may be subject to restrictive filtering that is preventing you from accessing Tor. In other words…

You are being blocked: Someone is actively breaking Tor to prevent you from connecting, for example, when China or Iran actively scans for Tor protocol network data and blocks it.

It can sometimes be difficult to differentiate between "you are being blocked" and "something is broken," because the end state—not being able to connect to Tor—looks the same in either case. The same goes for detecting the difference between "something has been broken by an active attacker" and "something has been broken by some benign mistake or bug."

This is why it is a good idea to get practice using Tor in a relatively forgiving or open network, where there are no active adversaries working to thwart you.

For more resources, consider these links:

- Query the Tor bug tracker (https://trac.torproject.org/projects/tor/query);
- Tor Project mailing lists (https://lists.torproject.org/cgi-bin/mailman/listinfo).

However, if you are on a network where Tor is being blocked, you will need to get a bridge relay.

4.2 BRIDGE RELAYS

Bridge relays (or "bridges" for short) are Tor relays that aren't listed in the main directory. Since there is no complete public list of them, even if your ISP is filtering connections to all the known Tor relays, they probably won't be able to block all the bridges.

A Tor bridge relay is usually specified as an IP address and port number (following the word bridge), as in this example:

```
bridge 172.16.27.48:443
```

Bridge listings usually begin with the word bridge, and can also include a modifier between bridge and the IP address. For example:

```
bridge obfs3 172.16.27.48:420
```

The modifier specifies a pluggable transport to be used with the bridge; in this case, obfs3 specifies the Tor protocol obfuscation layer, which is intended to make Tor traffic *not* look like Tor traffic (see below for more about pluggable transports).

Bridge listings may also sometimes be shown with an optional cryptographic element: the *fingerprint* of the bridge's public key. This permits authentication, but is not necessary for most users to have direct access to when setting up to use Tor bridges, because the Tor network protocol usually handles authentication transparently to the user. It looks like this:

```
bridge obfs2 10.21.27.48:420
4352e58420e68f5e40bf7c74faddccd9d1349413
```

Because the whole point of using a bridge is to have an entry point to the Tor network that isn't easily detected by a firewall operator, you can acquire bridge addresses, a few at a time, by e-mail or through your web browser.

For full details, see the "Tor bridges specification" document (https://gitweb.torproject.org/torspec.git?a = blob_plain;hb = HEAD; f = attic/bridges-spec.txt).

4.2.1 Getting a Bridge Relay Using BridgeDB

The Tor Project maintains a web interface to their BridgeDB database of bridge relays here:

```
https://bridges.torproject.org/
```

The page displays a brief explanation of Tor bridges and a CAPTCHA challenge–response you can enter to receive a short list of Tor bridges.

The page should also display a note (at the bottom) about using IPv6 addresses. This option is useful only if your system is configured for IPv6.

There is also an option to request *obfsproxy bridges*, bridges that support the use of obfsproxy, a way to transform Tor traffic into a format that looks like some other protocol (to prevent it from being blocked by a firewall). Obfsproxy and pluggable transports are discussed later in this chapter.

4.2.2 Getting Bridge Relays by E-mail

If you are unable to reach the Tor Project page to request bridge relays, you can also send an e-mail to a Tor Project e-mail robot that will send you bridge relay addresses. To get bridge relays by e-mail, send a message to the address:

```
bridges@bridges.torproject.org
```

The body of the message should be:

```
get bridges
```

Currently, the e-mail alias should respond to your request only if your e-mail came from a Yahoo! or Gmail account. This makes it more difficult for adversaries to learn the identity of more than a few unpublished bridge relays because Google and Yahoo! make it difficult to create lots of fake e-mail addresses. Using Gmail or Yahoo is also required/recommended because they both use HTTPS, which means your message will be encrypted and an attacker should not be able to detect that you are communicating with Tor, requesting bridge relays, or what those relays are in the reply.

The response from the Tor Project will look something like this (Figure 4.1):

4.2.3 Other Ways to Get Bridge Relays

If you are unable to get a bridge relay by e-mail or web, you may need to resort to more personal options. If you are able to communicate with someone who does have access to Tor, you can ask them to set up their Tor system as a bridge relay and give you their IP address/ port. Alternately, you may also (if it is possible) get in touch with the Tor Project in some way (by e-mail, through their website, or through a Tor mailing list) and someone may be able to help you out.

4.3 SETTING UP TO USE A BRIDGE RELAY

Once you have a Tor bridge address, go to the "Settings/Network" panel in Vidalia and click "My ISP blocks connections to the Tor network". Then add each bridge address, as shown in Figure 4.2 (note that the bridge addresses shown in this illustration are not valid bridge relays).

Configuring more than one bridge address will make your Tor connection more stable, in case one or more of the bridges you are using become unreachable.

```
[This is an automated message; please do not reply.]

Here are your bridge relays:

   bridge 10.71.137.223:443
   bridge 172.16.94.243:443
   bridge 192.168.96.125:9001
```

Figure 4.1 The response from the Tor Project's bridges@bridges.torproject.org *e-mail robot will look something like this. Note that the bridge addresses are examples only, and do not represent actual bridges.*

Figure 4.2 Adding bridges to your Tor configuration, via the Vidalia control panel. The bridge addresses shown are not valid Tor bridges, and should be considered examples only.

Currently, you may also request IPv6 bridges or bridges that support specific pluggable transports by using these commands in the body of the e-mail (instead of `bridges`):

```
ipv6            : request ipv6 bridges.
transport NAME : request transport NAME. Example: 'transport obfs2'
```

Other transports are being developed, see "Tor: Pluggable Transports" (https://www.torproject.org/docs/pluggable-transports.html. en) for the most up-to-date information about available transports.

4.4 PLUGGABLE TRANSPORTS AND OBFSPROXY

The simplest type of firewall works similarly to an ordinary network router, accepting packets from hosts on one "side" of the wall, and forwarding them as appropriate, based on the IP (network) addresses they are being sent to/from. In other words, if I attempt to send a message to a host that my adversary considers forbidden, the firewall will simply drop my packets rather than sending them to their destination.

An adversary can configure their firewall to drop packets being sent to/from known Tor relays, by hooking up to Tor themselves and downloading the list of public Tor relays. This attack can be circumvented by using bridge relays, as just described above—but there are more sophisticated ways to filter traffic.

Deep packet inspection (DPI) is one of those more sophisticated firewall techniques. In addition to blocking traffic to or from known Tor relays, a DPI firewall can be configured to look deeper into the network packets, beyond the source and the destination addresses. With DPI, the firewall examines other parts of packet headers, as well as the way the packet is formed and formatted. Using DPI, the adversary can detect Tor data and block it, even if it is being sent to a bridge relay.

Worse, the adversary can now start blocking access to any destination that has been known to send/receive Tor traffic, thus reducing or even eliminating that bridge's usefulness.

To circumvent these DPI firewalls (which includes the GFC), the Tor Project devised *pluggable transports*. From the Pluggable Transports web page (https://www.torproject.org/docs/pluggable-transports.html.en):

> Pluggable transports transform the Tor traffic flow between the client and the bridge. This way, censors who monitor traffic between the client and the bridge will see innocent-looking transformed traffic instead of the actual Tor traffic. External programs can talk to Tor clients and Tor bridges using the pluggable transport API, to make it easier to build interoperable programs.

In other words, using a pluggable transport enables the digital equivalent of the smuggler's trick of putting contraband inside something more innocent-looking item, like sewing diamonds inside a teddy bear. The pluggable transport programming interface makes it possible for developers to produce tools that obfuscate the Tor packets to make them appear to be innocent web traffic.

Unlike ordinary Tor, to connect to Tor via a pluggable transport proxy, you've got to have a version of Tor that supports network communication over the pluggable transport—meaning that a different version of the TBB is required. See below for more about how to accomplish this.

4.4.1 Pluggable Transport Proxies

Though virtually unpronounceable, the portmanteau word "obfsproxy" comes from "obfuscated proxy," and refers to a censorship circumvention tool that attempts to transform Tor traffic between the client and the bridge so that it looks like otherwise ordinary Internet traffic.

As of this writing, there are two transport proxies currently deployed for use with Tor: Obfsproxy (https://www.torproject.org/projects/obfsproxy.html.en), and flash proxy (http://crypto.stanford.edu/flashproxy/), both are included in the "obfsproxy" version of TBB.

Obfsproxy is the software framework within which pluggable transports are implemented. In other words, to use a pluggable transport, you'll need the obfsproxy version of the TBB (download from https://www.torproject.org/projects/obfsproxy.html.en#download). Obfsproxy supports two types of pluggable transport, so far, obfs2 and obfs3.

There are other transport proxies in development, including these, as described on the Tor Project page on Pluggable Transports (https://www.torproject.org/docs/pluggable-transports.html.en):

- *StegoTorus*: an Obfsproxy fork that extends it to (a) split Tor streams across multiple connections to avoid packet size signatures and (b) embed the traffic flows in traces that look like html, JavaScript, or pdf. (https://gitweb.torproject.org/stegotorus.git).
- *SkypeMorph*: transforms Tor traffic flows so they look like Skype Video (http://cacr.uwaterloo.ca/techreports/2012/cacr2012-08.pdf).
- *Dust*: aims to provide a packet-based (rather than connection-based) DPI-resistant protocol (https://github.com/blanu/Dust).
- *Format-Transforming Encryption*: transforms Tor traffic to arbitrary formats using their language descriptions (https://eprint.iacr.org/2012/494).

If and when these projects are deemed useful and useable, they are likely to be incorporated into the TBB in some form.

4.4.2 Flash Proxy

Flash proxy provides a way to turn anyone's web browser into a miniature proxy that can be used by anyone needing access to Tor. "Flash" originally referred to Adobe Flash, which is no longer a part of Flash proxy; instead, think of "flash" as referring to something that winks in and out of existence very quickly.

Here's how it works: if you can publish a web page, you can add a flash proxy "badge" to that page. The badge links to the flash proxy JavaScript code, which then turns your computer into an ephemeral proxy server. Your browser can be used as a flash proxy, but only as long as that page (the one with the badge) is being visited by your browser.

Flash proxy is currently included with the experimental (as of this writing) *Obfsproxy Tor Browser Bundle* (https://www.torproject.org/projects/obfsproxy.html.en#download); so if you use Obfsproxy, it is possible for you to use these flash proxies to connect to Tor. However, it can be a little complicated since you will probably need to configure your system to do port forwarding. Check the Flash Proxy Howto (https://trac.torproject.org/projects/tor/wiki/FlashProxyHowto) for the most up-to-date instructions for using flash proxy.

4.4.3 Using Pluggable Transports

First, download the Obfsproxy TBB (from https://www.torproject.org/projects/obfsproxy.html.en#download), validate the download's digital signature, and extract/install as appropriate for your OS.

From there, Tor should be functionally identical to "regular" Tor. Starting Tor will open Vidalia and the Tor Browser, after initializing on the Tor network—but with the difference being that the Tor network is accessed through obfsproxy bridges, rather than to a regular bridge, or directly via the Internet without any obfuscation. See Figure 4.3 for examples of how obfsproxy bridges are shown in the Tor configuration.

If you have trouble getting an obfsproxy bridge, you can use the same techniques (e-mail or web) described earlier in this chapter to get obfsproxy bridge addresses.

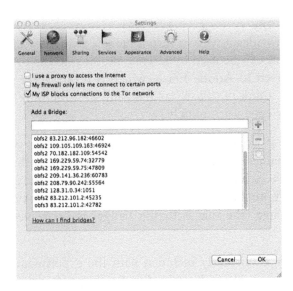

Figure 4.3 When using obfsproxy to bypass DPI, obfsproxy bridges are used, as shown in the Vidalia Settings/ Network panel.

CHAPTER 5

Sharing Tor Resources

This chapter explains how people can share their resources with others to access the Tor anonymity network and discusses the issues and risks involved with doing so.

5.1 HOW (AND WHY) I SHOULD CONTRIBUTE SERVICES

The more computers are connected through the Tor network, the better the network works: with more hosts passing Tor network data around the Internet, the less likely any one Tor user will be identified out of that mass of connecting computers.

Connecting to Tor and offering to share your connection as an exit relay, a transit relay, or a bridge is a good way to share your excess network bandwidth—as long as it is permitted under the terms of your ISP account. If it is allowed, you may find it gratifying to know that you may be helping political activists to communicate safely—or that your bandwidth may have carried diplomatic communiques from remote parts of the world.

However, the most efficient way to contribute bandwidth is by donating cash to a charity that runs exit relays. These two are currently operating:

- *torservers.net* (https://www.torservers.net): a German charitable non-profit that runs a wide variety of exit relays and
- *Noisebridge* (https://www.noisebridge.net/wiki/Noisebridge_Tor): an US-based 501(c)(3) nonprofit that accepts donations to expand exit relay capacity.

If you are confident in your system/network management skills and are not restricted by ISP terms of use, then consider configuring your system to act as a Tor relay.

5.2 WHAT ARE YOUR OPTIONS

When configuring as a relay, there are two important configuration options:

- Is exiting to the public Internet permitted?
- Is the relay publicized as a bridge relay or as a regular relay?

First, a bit about the second configuration option. There are two separate protocol structures for distributing relay addresses on the Tor network: there is a *bridge authority* which manages all the addresses for Tor bridge relays, and then the normal Tor *directory authority* that manages addresses for all regular Tor relays (transit or exit).

So, the different relay options (bridge, exit, or transit) can be characterized by what they allow:

- *Exit relay*: a relay that permits exiting to the public Internet, and that is published to the normal directory authorities. Exit relays may be used in any position in a Tor circuit (as the first or second hops) but only exit relays may be used for the last hop in a Tor circuit.
- *Transit relay*: a relay that does not permit exiting to the public Internet, but that is published to the normal directory authorities. Transit relays may be used only for the first or second hops in a Tor circuit. These may also be called *middle* or *nonexit* nodes.
- *Bridge*: a relay that is published only to the Tor bridge authority. A bridge relay can be used only in the first hop of a Tor circuit, only for Tor clients configured to use that bridge.

You can configure your Tor connection for sharing from the Vidalia control panel: clicking on the shortcut labeled "Setup Relaying" will take you to the Settings/Sharing panel in Vidalia (see Figure 5.1).

The choices are to run a nonexit (transit) relay, run an exit relay, or to run a bridge relay:

- *Exit relay*: a Tor node that permits forwarding from the Tor network to the public Internet. Exit relays know the IP addresses of the services being accessed through Tor, but no way to link them to the Tor client accessing them. Someone monitoring your network could detect your presence as a Tor exit node, and would also be able to

Figure 5.1 Configuring Tor relaying options in the Vidalia control program.

identify the services being accessed through Tor—but not the Tor clients accessing them.

- *Nonexit relay*: a Tor node that accepts Tor network traffic from other Tor nodes, including Tor clients and other Tor transit relays. Someone monitoring your network could detect your presence as a Tor transit node, but all Tor network traffic is encrypted and inaccessible to anyone with access to your system or network.
- *Bridge relay*: a Tor node that accepts Tor network traffic from Tor clients seeking to establish the first hop in a Tor circuit only. Tor users can get bridge relays by web or e-mail (see Chapter 4). Since your IP address is not publicly linked or advertised as being a Tor relay, any firewall that blocks public Tor relays should not block your relay. If the firewall does deep packet inspection, your identity as a Tor relay could be compromised. Although an adversary monitoring your network would be able to identify you as a Tor relay, as well as identify the IP addresses of Tor clients using your relay, they would not be able to determine where those Tor clients are connecting on the public Internet.

Which option to choose? From the Tor Project website (https:// www.torproject.org/docs/faq.html.en#RelayOrBridge):

So should you run a normal relay or bridge relay? If you have lots of bandwidth, you should definitely run a normal relay. If you're willing to be an exit, you should definitely run a normal relay, since we need more exits. If you can't be an exit and only have a little bit of bandwidth, be a bridge. Thanks for volunteering!

5.3 WHAT DO YOU RISK

Contributing network resources to Tor has a downside (the upside being the feeling of fulfillment one gets from doing a good deed): no good deed goes unpunished. But seriously, the risks fall into three categories:

• Abuse complaints;
• Cost of bandwidth;
• ISP may not like it.

It should go without saying that if you donate resources in these ways to Tor, you will find that some of your network bandwidth and your system capacity are now being used for Tor connectivity. This may cost you (if you pay per unit of bandwidth rather than a fixed rate for "unlimited" service); as noted, some ISPs prefer that their customers not use their bandwidth to support Tor. To avoid problems, be sure to consult with your ISP or network services provider prior to configuring your system as a relay of any type.

That leaves the issue of abuse complaints. For full details, see "So what should I expect if I run an exit relay?" (https://www.torproject.org/docs/faq-abuse.html.en#TypicalAbuses). Mostly, because your system is acting on behalf of other systems, if some anonymous user connects to a Gmail account through your exit relay, and if that account is being monitored by a law enforcement agency for some reason, that would link your IP address with that Gmail account—and you would have to explain that you are running a Tor exit node.

If you are a system administrator, responding to such issues can be automated fairly easily, but most regular users will probably prefer to avoid the issue entirely.

Alternatively, you can configure your exit relay to reject traffic that might cause problems for you.

5.4 CONFIGURING AS A TOR RELAY

The first step to configuring your system as a Tor relay is to get Tor running. You should be able to configure your system as a Tor relay with "regular" Tor as well as with Tor running over obfsproxy (see Chapter 4).

Setting up as a Tor relay of any kind calls for more technical knowledge than using Tor, and possibly not worthwhile if you are running Tor for short sessions on a personal computer. To set up as a relay ordinarily would mean that you are making a commitment to running for a relatively long time, for example, for days/weeks/months even, rather than for a few hours at a time.

However, there may be circumstances under which it would be useful or helpful to run a more ephemeral relay, particularly if you know someone who needs an otherwise unknown bridge relay (see below). The first thing to do is consider system requirements and the possible consequences of running as a Tor relay, then, having decided what type of relay to run, walk through the configuration process as described below.

5.5 REQUIREMENTS AND CONSEQUENCES

The current basic requirements for running a Tor relay are that your system should have reliable network access, with a minimum of 20 KBps bandwidth available for Tor traffic. Once your relay has been fully integrated into the Tor network infrastructure, you may find that it uses a lot of network bandwidth, so that should be kept in mind as well.

Before configuring your relay, you should spend some time reading up on how to do it safely, as well as how to deal with problems that may arise while your system is a Tor relay.

Number one, most of the time it is not a good idea to run a relay on your home network: it may violate your ISP's acceptable use policies, it may cause a large spike in your network usage (and possible increase in fees or loss of service), and it may also complicate matters to mix Tor relay traffic with your own personal network use. To start, see the article, "Tips for Running an Exit Node with Minimal Harassment" (https://blog.torproject.org/blog/tips-running-exit-node-minimal-harassment).

Ideally, then, your Tor relay will be on a separate network and system from the one you normally use, it should be connected through an ISP that allows such use, and it should have a reliable network connection with sufficient bandwidth to be useful to the network. Up to now, the absolute minimum available bandwidth acceptable to act as a relay is

20 KBps; however, to be useful, a relay should be able to provide, at a minimum, 50 KBps of available bandwidth (keeping in mind that the Tor Project will likely be increasing the official minimum in the near future).

Finally, before running a Tor transit or exit relay, it is recommended that you start out by running a bridge relay because they do not require quite as much bandwidth to be helpful, and they have a lower impact to the person running the relay.

5.6 NONEXIT RELAY

To configure as a Tor nonexit relay, from the Vidalia Settings/Sharing panel (see Figure 5.1), select the "Relay traffic inside the Tor network (nonexit relay)" option. From there, you can configure the basic settings:

- *Nickname*: a name by which your relay is known on the network. While optional, a nickname is especially useful if you manage more than one relays.
- *Contact Info*: an e-mail address (plus an OpenPGP key ID or fingerprint, if desired/available). While optional, you would only be contacted if there is an important security update to Tor, or if there is an issue with your relay.
- *Relay Port*: the port number on which your system listens for Tor network requests. The default is 9001, but if that is blocked, some other port (often, port 443) would be used.
- *Mirror the Relay Directory/Directory Port*: mirroring the Tor directory means that your relay acts as a resource for Tor clients looking for information about all the other Tor relays, so that the client can create its Tor circuits. This is an option for a transit or exit relay, but directory mirroring is required for bridge relays. The port number must be different from the Tor relay port (see above), and is port 9030, by default.
- *Attempt to automatically configure port forwarding*: The "Test" button is part of this option, and tests for the ability to automatically configure port forwarding. Port forwarding is required for relays that are behind routers/firewalls that would ordinarily hide and prevent inbound network access to your system.

There is a second active configuration panel for setting bandwidth limits. The default options allow you to specify a portion of your high-speed Internet access be made available for Tor traffic; the minimum default choice is 256 KBps; if that is too much—or the maximum, greater than 1.5 MBps, too little—you can configure a custom average/maximum bandwidth you are willing to commit to Tor uses.

5.7 EXIT NODE

Configuring as an exit node raises more issues, as your system is in direct contact with the servers a Tor client is trying to reach. This could be a problem if those servers are being used for objectionable purposes, as your IP address is the one connected to the activity on those servers.

Configuring an exit relay is identical to configuring a transit/nonexit relay, with the addition of the option to configure Exit Policies. Configuring exit policies is how you limit what kind of server the Tor clients using your relay are able to connect to. For example, by limiting access to "Secure Websites (SSL)," your relay will only forward network traffic intended for websites that support HTTPS. Other traffic will not be accepted.

Exit policies are part of the relay information that your system advertises to the Tor network, so users trying to reach an e-mail server would have to find a different Tor exit relay for such a connection, in the event that those protocols are blocked.

By disabling *all* exit protocols, you effectively turn your Tor exit relay into a nonexit relay—much simpler to just specify that when first configuring as a relay. While it is most desirable (and useful for the Tor network) to operate an exit relay that supports as many protocols as possible, not everyone who shares their system resources is willing or able to do so. Being an entry-only relay is still useful to the Tor network, and worth doing—as is being a HTTPS-only exit relay, which can reduce some of your exposure by requiring that all traffic forwarded to the public Internet is encrypted (with HTTPS).

5.8 BRIDGE RELAY

Configuring a bridge relay is similar to exit/transit relays, but with the addition of being able to control how your bridge address is distributed. So you configure the Basic Settings and the Bandwidth Limits—but you don't need to configure Exit Policies.

The big difference is that you have the option of automatically distributing your bridge relay's address, by checking/unchecking the box at the bottom of the Sharing panel. Also, once your bridge relay is initialized (by clicking the OK button after configuring), the system generates a line of text that can be used to identify your bridge. It looks like this:

```
10.110.171.18:9001  F5C81437057BCD0C58AE50079DD788045B3A9AFE
^                   ^    ^
IP address      Port Fingerprint
```

The first line above shows an example of the bridge address. (*Note*: This is not an actual valid bridge relay address, but this is what it would look like.)

The first part is the IP address, with port number (9001), followed by a 40-byte fingerprint used to authenticate the bridge cryptographically.

If you are setting up a bridge relay for a particular person who needs one, you can pass along this string of data to that person, who can then configure their Tor client to use the bridge. This allows you to help someone, without having to distribute your bridge address to anyone but the person who needs it (assuming you have a secure channel over which to share with that person).

This is one way that people with good access to the Tor network can help individuals behind national firewalls that do deep packet inspection.

CHAPTER 6

Tor Hidden Services

One natural by-product of creating an anonymization network protocol like that used by Tor is that it makes it possible for a node that exists on the network to act not just as a client (e.g., for browsing websites on the public Internet anonymously) but also to act as a server. A server that can be accessed by other clients within the anonymity network, while the actual location (IP address) of the server remains anonymous.

When using Tor to maintain anonymity as a client while accessing the global Internet, the Tor network itself (comprising all those systems set up to act as Tor relays) functions (for the user) like a simple network proxy.

The user in those cases doesn't access anything connected to the Tor anonymity network, except Tor relays. This actually implies that there is (and must be) a Tor networking protocol capable of supporting basic networking functions (directory services, routing protocols) and data formats, and the rest of the infrastructure to allow systems to communicate anonymously—whether they are acting as clients or servers. This is how the anonymization network produces as a by-product the ability to run a server, anonymously.

6.1 WHY? WHY PEOPLE WANT TO USE HIDDEN SERVICES

The first question about Tor hidden services is usually about "good" uses for Tor hidden services; this is probably the result of the amount of media coverage given to Tor hidden services that are used to break laws, fueled by calls for regulation of Tor by frustrated politicians and law enforcement officials.

Why speak of "good" (or "bad") here? Like any tool, Tor hidden services are not in themselves inherently good or bad, but they can be used to achieve good or bad ends. While hidden services can be (and are) used by criminals, they are also used by those working on behalf of human rights, personal freedom, and safety for victims of abuse.

The difference is that if there were no Tor network, criminals are willing and able to commit crimes to further their activities by stealing mobile phones, hacking e-mail accounts, identity theft, and more. Law-abiding citizens do not have these options to secure their own personal privacy.

Any service that can be published to the Internet can be hosted as a Tor hidden service, though most commonly people set up a web server to run as a hidden web server. You could also set up e-mail, file transfer, or chat servers as hidden services.

Tor Project's page, "Using Tor hidden services for good" (https://blog. torproject.org/blog/using-tor-good), is a good place to start for some suggested applications, and for understanding the valuable benefits of using them. Here is a short overview of some of those "good" uses:

- People in areas where state-sponsored attacks prevent them from blogging freely. One solution is to have someone outside the region host a hidden server for submitting new content to the blog, and publish that content on the public Internet as static HTML.
- Mirroring a news or activist site as a hidden service means that even if a government attempts to shut down the site, the hidden service mirror will still be accessible (to Tor users, at least).
- Hidden services are useful for those interested in publishing or collecting information from whistle-blowers, without being subject to prior restraint or complete censorship by organizations or governments that may not approve of the publication of unflattering information. See for example http://globaleaks.org/ or https://wiki-leaks.org/.

Other possible good uses for Tor hidden services would include chat or other social media services that cannot track individual users and that provide a forum for unimpeded free speech in parts of the world where governments or corporations would prefer to monitor and censor such speech.

6.2 HOW TOR HIDDEN SERVICES WORK

To run a Tor hidden server, the first requirement is that the system be connected to the Tor network. While there are ways to access Tor hidden services without using Tor, they do not offer any anonymity or security to the user (see Section 6.2.3).

Anonymity of the publisher begins with the server being a Tor network node (connected to the Tor network anonymously). Even so, there is still a network address (an anonymous address) associated with the (anonymously) connected computer: if I know *this* address, I can connect to the web or e-mail server running on that computer, wherever it happens to be and whoever is hosting it.

It's worthwhile to think of the Tor network as an abstraction, simply a medium through which nodes communicate anonymously. Doing so allows you to ignore the details of the creation of Tor circuits, and more easily visualize the interactions between the various anonymous nodes.

6.2.1 The Tor Hidden Service Protocol

The Tor Hidden Service Protocol (see https://www.torproject.org/docs/hidden-services.html) describes how Tor hidden services work. When setting up a Tor hidden service, the hidden server chooses, at random, three Tor relays to be used as *introduction points*. The hidden server creates separate Tor circuits for each of these relays: three separate and complete Tor circuits, so that none of the introduction points are connected to the same IP addresses, but the hidden server is still uniquely identifiable through cryptographic means. It doesn't matter what IP address the server is hiding behind, the hidden server can, and does, prove its identity cryptographically—by using its own secret key to demonstrate that it is the owner of the *pseudo-URL* (also known as the *onion address*) derived from the server's public key.

Once those three Tor circuits are in place, the hidden server can publish the data necessary to connect: the introduction points and the identifying data required to cryptographically assure that communications directed to that hidden service arrive there.

The hidden server registers this data with the systems hosting the *hidden service directory database.* When someone wants to connect to the hidden service, they send a request to this database, which then directs them to one of the hidden service's introduction points. From there, the Tor client and the hidden server negotiate a circuit through a *rendezvous point*. At this point, the client has three Tor relays between it and the rendezvous point, and the hidden server is similarly buffered by three Tor relays between itself and its rendezvous point.

In other words, it goes like this:

```
Tor client <==>
    Tor entry relay <==>
        Tor transit relay <==>
            Tor transit relay <==>
                <==> RENDEZVOUS POINT <==>
            Tor transit relay <==>
        Tor transit relay <==>
    Tor entry relay <==>
hidden server
```

The introduction points know the client and server only through their anonymized Tor circuits; the client and server then negotiate further anonymity by using the introduction point only long enough to set up the rendezvous point. The rendezvous point will be different every time the client and server connect, so it becomes difficult/impossible to link a hidden service with a location by monitoring and comparing network traffic. And even the introduction points have no way of linking the hidden server with an IP address, because the introduction points point only to the Tor transit nodes through which the hidden service is connected, not the hidden server itself.

6.2.2 Onion Pseudo-URLs

Tor hidden services are not directly addressable from the global/public Internet: instead of a standard Internet domain name (like example. com or example.org), they must use what is known as a pseudo-URL. Tor hidden service names sort of look like ordinary domain names, but rather than using a global Internet top-level domain (like .com, .edu, .de, or .info) they end in .onion (pronounced "dot-onion" and referring to the origins of the Tor project, onion routing).

The first part of the domain name is a 16-character string (numbers and letters only) that is derived from the hidden service's public key (see section 6.3, "How to Set Up a Tor HIdden Service", for more on page 95). These names appear randomly, and are necessary so that the hidden server can respond to requests by authenticating themselves using their secret key to demonstrate they are, indeed, the holder of the public key linked to that 16-byte service name.

See Table 6.1 for some examples of Tor hidden services and their Tor addresses.

The .onion domain names form the pseudo-URLs in the same way that public Internet domain names are used to make URLs. So to reach a nonweb service, like file transfer protocol (FTP), you would create a pseudo-URL like this:

```
ftp://kj22ic3odyoqeac7.onion
```

Also, to address a page on a .onion website, you would add the directory/filename the same as with a standard URL:

```
http://kj22ic3odyoqeac7.onion/blog/this-is-a-blog-entry-title
```

Note that hidden services aren't usually published as HTTPS sites, because to do so would require setting up a cryptographic certificate, which might compromise anonymity for the publisher. Also, because (of course) content sent to and from a hidden service is already encrypted sufficiently to protect against network monitoring—exactly the purpose of using HTTPS (see sidebar, "HTTP Secure and HTTPS Everywhere", on page 15).

6.2.3 Web-to-Onion Proxies

The Tor network is just that, a network—the same as the global Internet is a network. When someone wants to connect from one network to another, there must, first, be a physical network connection: a wireless network, a physical cable link, or a special system that has physical connections to both networks.

Table 6.1 Some Examples of Tor Hidden Services and Their Tor Addresses	
Description	**Hidden Service**
The Tor Project website, hosted as a hidden service	`http://idnxcnkne4qt76tg.onion/`
Tor Project package archive of all software released by Tor Project	`http://j6im4v42ur6dpic3.onion/`
Tor Project official bug tracker and wiki site	`http://vwp5zrdfwmw4avcq.onion/`
Tor Project official media archive: all Tor images, videos, and related files	`http://p3igkncehackjtib.onion/`
Duck Duck Go (anonymous web searching)	`http://3g2upl4pq6kufc4m.onion/`
New Yorker Strongbox, for anonymously s ubmitting files or messages to New Yorker magazine staff	`http://tnysbtbxsf356hiy.onion`
Note that the Tor Project hidden service hosts the exact same website as hosted at torproject.org, which means that links to other Tor Project websites (such as the Tor Project bug tracker/wiki and the Tor Project blog) point to the public Internet, not the .onion versions of those sites; see below for those addresses.	

If the systems on both networks use the same set of protocols to determine how data is exchanged, such as TCP/IP for networks like the Internet, then interoperability requires only the network connection and the common protocols.

However, the Tor network uses a different set of protocols (the Tor protocols), which run on top of TCP/IP; the Internet uses TCP/IP alone. To connect to a Tor hidden service, you would need to run Tor—OR, you could connect via Internet to a system that is connected both to the Tor network and the Internet.

There are a number of websites that do just that: they accept a Tor hidden service, .onion address, and act as a proxy to that service.

Some onion proxy services include:

- tor2web (http://tor2web.org/);
- Onion.to (http://onion.to/);
- Onion.sh (https://onion.sh/).

While this type of Tor hidden service proxy can be convenient for quickly taking a peek at hidden services, they do not provide any real protection for the user, and may represent an extra risk, in that the operators of these proxy websites may retain information from your sessions with the hidden servers. The publishers of the hidden services are still shielded, but your activity on those sites will be relatively easy for an adversary to monitor and link to you.

6.2.4 Turning Over the Rocks

There are probably quite a few hidden services floating around the Tor network. Some of them are "open for business" and seek new users, others are there to provide a service of some sort for individuals or groups, and others are published as a way for their publishers to "leave a mark", shock, or otherwise offend or disturb.

If you go looking for hidden servers just to surf, as you would in the public Internet, you are far more likely to find things that offend you, including offensive images, offensive viewpoints, and sites that promote/sell criminal products and services. Also, copyright infringement and scams are all around.

For example, consider one of the more notorious hidden services: the Silk Road drug trading website. You can easily find the correct . onion address for Silk Road on the public Internet (`silkroadvb5piz3r. onion`), but you will also find scam sites whose .onion pseudo-URLs are similar to that address but which point to login pages used to phish Silk Road users' login information.

Since there is no central authority, no rules and no way to enforce them on Tor hidden services, be particularly wary when accessing any hidden service—the people behind it can do anything they like, with impunity.

6.3 HOW TO SET UP A TOR HIDDEN SERVICE

Conceptually, setting up a Tor hidden service is simply a matter of setting up a network service on a Tor client, and then modifying the configuration so that all access to that service is through the Tor network. This is comparable, at a technical level, to setting up a proprietary network storage system (like Novell's NetWare or Microsoft's Windows NT) to be accessible through the global Internet via TCP/IP.

For hidden services, the Tor networking software has to be set up to accept requests from the Tor network, and forward them (on the system hosting the hidden server) to the software running the network service (e.g., the standard TCP/IP server program, such as a web or mail server).

What this means is that if you plan on setting up a Tor hidden server, you should have the skills to set up a regular, nonhidden service on an Internet-connected server—plus the know-how to run a Tor client.

Setting up a Tor client to run a hidden service can be summarized in four steps (from "Configuring Hidden Services for Tor" (https://www. torproject.org/docs/tor-hidden-service.html.en)):

- Get Tor working.
- Install a server locally on the system running Tor.
- Configure the hidden service. A matter of adding two lines to the Tor configuration file (torrc).
- Tips and pointers and suggestions. In other words, it's not that easy.

If you have Tor working, and have a server on your Tor system, you can set up hidden services through the Vidalia control panel (see Figure 6.1). If you do this, you should consider it a first step; you may wish to do more system tweaking to make sure that your hidden service is truly hidden.

If you've got a web server configured on your system, and if you can install and run the Tor client software on your system, setting up a hidden service can be actually quite simple—but doing it securely and in a way that maximizes anonymity and reduces risks of exposure is not quite that simple.

6.3.1 Get Tor Working

As you may already know, from having used the Tor Browser Bundle or Tails, getting Tor running on your system can be quite simple. But the question missing from this instruction is, "where should I run my Tor hidden service?"

Best security practices suggest that you not run a hidden server on your home computer: doing so may attract attention, especially if your service gets a lot of traffic. An adversary may also be able to correlate up and down time of the hidden service to times that your computer is turned on/off. In other words, an attacker can monitor a hidden service

Figure 6.1 Configuring Tor hidden services using the Vidalia control panel.

and monitor your connectivity; if the hidden service goes down when you turn your computer off, it may be enough to accuse you of running that hidden service.

If you do plan to run a hidden service, you should take precautions to maintain anonymity in the face of whatever attacker you might be facing. Here are some options to consider (from notes published by Roger Dingledine, Tor project leader and one of the original developers of Tor):

- Run Tor on a *virtual machine* (VM), and make sure that the VM cannot discover the IP address or domain name of the system on which it is running. Running as a VM gives the system administrator more control over what the Tor client can and can't do.
- Run Tor on a *virtual private server* (VPS), and as Dingledine wrote, "put that VM in a VPS running in a country that hates my adversary. That way even if somebody breaks into the web server and breaks out of the VM, they're still faced with a frustratingly long bureaucratic step." This works best if the country hosting the VPS also has privacy-friendly legislation in place (and where officials and server hosting employees are not easily corrupted).

Doing this (a VM on a VPS in an unfriendly country) places multiple layers of security around the hidden server because:

- it is on a VM that can be encrypted, be power cycled, or even wiped remotely, and that has no way to know what IP address or domain name of the computer on which it is running;
- it is on a VPS, so it is just one of many VMs running out of the same physical hardware; this means an additional layer of complexity for an adversary to attempt to unravel and analyze traffic;
- it is on a VPS in a country unfriendly to the adversary (and presumably friendly to privacy concerns), which puts a bureaucratic obstacle in the way of any adversary.

So, now that you've got Tor installed, securely, the next issue is installing the server software.

6.3.2 Install a Server

Although the most common (and, therefore, the easiest to install using various tutorials and installer scripts) web server is Apache (http://httpd.apache.org/), this is not recommended for hosting anonymous services. Apache may be a bulletproof and ordinarily quite secure web server, it has also accumulated over time many great features, some of which might be subverted by an attacker.

In the article referenced above, Dingledine suggests that it is best to "run a good solid web server like nginx" (nginx, pronounced "engine-x", is an open source web server that is often used for hidden servers; see http://nginx.org/). Dingledine was careful *not* to say "use nginx," but rather to recommend something like it: open source, mature, widely used, and without too many bells and whistles which might introduce anonymity vulnerabilities that are not considered "security issues" for the vast majority of users (who are not on Tor).

Using a good, secure web server—one that you know how to run securely—adds another layer of security to those cited above: the first line of defense for a hidden service is the server.

6.3.3 Configure the Hidden Service

When you use Vidalia to set up a hidden service, it will generate the two lines you need to add to the Tor configuration file (torrc) for you, and start the service automatically. These lines will be something like:

```
HiddenServiceDir /Library/Tor/var/lib/tor/hidden_service/
HiddenServicePort 80 127.0.0.1:8080
```

For Windows users, something like this:

```
HiddenServiceDir C:\Users\username\Documents\tor\hidden_service
HiddenServicePort 80 127.0.0.1:8080
```

The first line here uses the HiddenServiceDir directive to point to the hidden service directory using a fully qualified directory. That directory is where you put the content for your hidden service.

The second line, using the HiddenServicePort directive, specifies (first) a *virtual* port (the port that users appear to be using to connect to your service) followed by the IP address:port that connections to the hidden service are *actually* using. In these examples, the virtual port is 80, the default for unsecured HTTP; and the address:port, 127.0.0.1:8080, points to the *loopback* address (an address that the computer interprets as "*This* computer") and port number 8080, an alternate port for web connections.

Generally, you would want to keep the hidden service address as the loopback address—it provides no deanonymizing information at all (referring, by definition, to the system running Tor). Port addresses may need to be changed depending on the hidden service being used (80, 443, and 8080 are all usually used for web servers; other types of servers use other ports, such as 25 for e-mail services, 20 for file transfer, and many others).

Once the new configuration is enabled (by restarting, or on first configuring through Vidalia), Tor automatically does some housekeeping chores:

- Tor generates a private/public key pair, and writes a file called "private_key" in the hidden service directory (see Figure 6.2).
- Tor generates a .onion pseudo-URL hostname for the hidden service, based on the public key of the private/public key pair.
- Tor writes a file called "hostname," which contains, on a single line, the .onion pseudo-URL hostname.

From the Vidalia hidden service configuration panel, you can click the third button from the top, on the right side of the panel, to copy the .onion address of a selected service to your system's clipboard. This makes it more convenient to accurately use or share that address.

6.3.4 Further Tips, Tricks, and Traps

No matter how you configure your hidden service, it is a good idea to take steps to ensure continuity as well as anonymity of your service.

If you want your hidden service to be available at a single .onion address over time—or if you are running your hidden service from a VM (strongly recommended)—you should back up and protect the private_key file (see Figure 6.2). This file contains a text-only version of your hidden service's secret cryptographic key; if an adversary gets access to this key they will be able to create a hacked version of your service, and users will not be able to determine whether they are connected to your server or your attacker's server.

Therefore, if you back up this key, you should do so in a way that makes it as difficult as possible for an adversary to recover it. You may prefer to encrypt it on a disc or thumb drive, and then store that

```
-----BEGIN RSA PRIVATE KEY-----
+cmMqNyiCMz4StSaiNRIXOgJm+a+4AHPJgFViaosg+ks/yvAqzU0h8HsTyTtNQKB
MIICXgIBAAKBgQDMopDdM2NXZl+snvFM3nSjaVFhx62yL0iZlf43eKMo+1C3NZvj
AoGBAJHpULYJEEqfmpSxeI1BDZX/YKICCR5GjNPGmc/f2yc65RbdyNxTnZ0IQtne
q0a/ewWqHKSm8Us0IbFzOS+djBVAbpwmmxJNAXkZrVk7AYwIDAQABY6v7uu5ATNe
8HfSisEr/2zwJhCczoFWqiGZoWDfpKXk3KrPMMDPVEIpTeM0BQpf2J5CihXPBn8B
KDQOt/XSwwJBAM94JOR9AJe0dcEtKB/06NX5v4C9fNiF07mg7uVaCjQxiDec/gnz
Pl30vO3pkR6j41iIR6YG5+TdnyvXh1qhivhA69dCqDgsRRo1zqxtx/O4WPrHAkBj
fCRyPxixah9hNMhvMxo4Pk5m855Ne7p/QeECQQCHYm2zZ5KqeGJJymNwLCT6gQqx
Ko/NaUOGIcamPlWCtTC34yUWWZ31LlaAhUd98BWBAkEA/ICyRXfDsTHYOSa3TbW2
XUgkGDfFAB3u3VOUPg54xhrIfzdcFzJjjVoR6fdX8NFpV7CjsNx5C6QiXX2oIWSI
eo1IrdQkqq1llwiGhjzhAkEA0BsD5OYdsU87LPw7CaV0ehJloU1lgrat/XE0jM4z
Z9R9aetjxMJ7CZDlJup8w8pe++uarxyQH6z3VVn4QhdbVixeRjygFeFninInkOLC
2tjuw5ggZRhIMZn7GfHM3pNhzVgerPx3yRi1cCS0ez9wYA==
-----END RSA PRIVATE KEY-----
```

Figure 6.2 The contents of the file `private_key` *will look something like this.*

media somewhere very safe; you may wish to print it out and store that copy somewhere safe. What you don't want to do is print out a copy and tack it to your office wall or save a copy of the key unencrypted on your computer.

You can run more than one hidden service on a single Tor client, simply by adding more HiddenServiceDir/HiddenServicePort configuration lines (see Figure 6.1, which shows two hidden services set up). If you do so, however, you will have to specify two different ports, so that your server will know which service is being requested on the local host.

If you are running a hidden service on a Tor client, you should run Tor as a client only; do not configure as a relay. Doing so will have performance impact on your service, but more importantly, running as a relay on the same system hosting a hidden service exposes a vulnerability that your adversary might be able to exploit. There are attacks that make it easier to locate a hidden server running on a Tor relay (but it is not a trivial attack, and has not yet been demonstrated to work on any actual hidden services).

For more about issues related to running a hidden service, see the article "Hidden services need some love" (https://blog.torproject.org/blog/hidden-services-need-some-love) on the Tor Project blog. This article is a must-read if you are setting up a hidden service and want to understand more about the risks and issues involved. Some of the issues noted relate to things like the difficulty of scaling a hidden service to support large numbers of users, problems with the protocols that enable certain types of denial of service (DoS) attacks, weaknesses in the protocol that make certain types of attacks feasible, and options for improving anonymity and performance.

CHAPTER 7

E-mail Security and Anonymity Practices

As noted in Chapter 1, David Petraeus was unable to secure his own secret e-mail communication. If the former director of the CIA has trouble figuring out how to keep himself anonymous, you can imagine that securing your e-mail might be more difficult than it at first seems.

Safe and anonymous e-mail is complicated by several factors:

- E-mail providers, whether they are your ISP or a webmail service like Google Mail or Yahoo! Mail, either already know who you are and where to find you (your ISP, for example), or else they want to know who you are and how to reach you. Webmail providers often require a backup e-mail address and/or a telephone number.
- E-mail providers can (and do) log the IP addresses from which you access your e-mail account, so if you are able to set up an anonymous e-mail account you should only access it anonymously using Tor—accessing it even once through the public Internet can give an adversary enough information to connect your real identity with your anonymous e-mail account.
- Not all webmail providers allow HTTPS access to e-mail accounts, so any messages exchanged with the server will be vulnerable to being sniffed from the Tor exit node to the webmail provider. HTTPS access is gaining ground, but before using any e-mail service it is important to verify that messages are encrypted end-to-end from the server to the client.
- Some webmail providers block account access or creation from Tor exit nodes. If you can't use Tor, some or all of your webmail activity can be monitored by (or through the services of) your ISP.
- Unless you encrypt all your messages and accept only encrypted messages—the mail you send and receive may be accessible to anyone with access to your mail provider's systems. Some mail providers encrypt your data—but they usually retain control over the encryption keys, so an adversary with sufficient influence (or a subpoena) can see the plaintext of your messages.

This chapter discusses why and how to use e-mail anonymously with Tor, and how to avoid at least some of these vulnerabilities.

There are different ways to use e-mail, so there are different ways to reduce your e-mail trail depending on why you want to use it anonymously.

One issue to keep in mind is that e-mail anonymity is not the same as e-mail pseudonymity. In some cases, people want to be able to use an e-mail address exactly once: either to simply send a message to a recipient without possibility of getting a reply, or to send a message and receive a single reply.

In this chapter, we'll consider four different approaches to e-mail anonymity/pseudonymity, as well as the reasons and how to use each approach.

7.1 ONE-TIME (THROWAWAY) ACCOUNTS

Sometimes, you'd like to be able to join/register with a website or service—to be able to post news, make comments, or interact with others online in some other way. Most websites require an e-mail address, in part to protect themselves (so that scammers don't automate the process of creating new accounts for malicious purposes) but also so that they can identify their members—and to communicate with them, and perhaps even to sell their e-mail addresses and/or user data to third parties.

You can often avoid giving a real e-mail address (one that links to your real identity) by using a throwaway e-mail address. Often referred to as a temporary or disposable address, throwaways can be acquired from various websites in many different forms. For example, consider these examples of some of the different services now online:

7.1.1 10minutemail.com

This site provides a single e-mail address on the home page, which you can give to someone else—like a nosy website that wants a valid e-mail address for your registration. The page updates periodically to display any messages sent to that account. As should be obvious from the site name, the e-mail address is only valid for 10 minutes, unless you request additional time. Once the time is up, your e-mail address (and messages) disappears (apparently).

Some problems with this service include:

- You must trust that whoever controls this site is not logging your IP address OR any messages received through their service.
- This site does not have HTTPS support, so your temporary e-mail address, as well as any messages you receive at that address, can be easily monitored in plaintext by anyone on your local network.
- If your traffic is logged by your ISP, it will be obvious that you've used this service (unless you access through Tor).
- Some sites try to track the domains used by temporary e-mail sites like this one, and block users from registering accounts using them.

7.1.2 Anonymous E-mail (http://www.5ymail.com/)

This site allows you to send a message and/or a file attachment, "anonymously." However, one of their "features" is a service that notifies you when your message was read. You must give a valid e-mail address to use this service, thus very likely nullifying any anonymity you might have had.

This service has many of the same drawbacks noted for 10minute-mail.com, with the additional problem that you can choose to send your message for free—if you allow an advertisement to be attached to the message. This notifies your recipient (and anyone who is monitoring *their* mail) that you used this service to send the message, giving your adversary a place to start deanonymizing you. Otherwise, you've got to pay for the message—which also deanonymizes you through the link to your credit card/PayPal account.

7.1.3 Avoid These Services

Anything you send to or receive from this type of "anonymous" e-mail service is vulnerable to being viewed by the service provider, even if you use Tor to connect to the provider. The provider is generally under no obligation to protect your information, and you should carefully check the terms and conditions under which they offer the service.

If you are using this type of e-mail address to give to a webmail provider (for example, Gmail) as a "backup" or "emergency" e-mail address, you should be aware that the confirmation messages sent by the webmail provider may be vulnerable to being sniffed (if the throwaway e-mail provider does not use HTTPS) on your local network—as well as being vulnerable to anyone with access to the throwaway e-mail provider's servers—even if you use Tor to get the account.

This type of service will not protect your identity from a truly determined adversary, and should probably be avoided unless absolutely necessary. There are better options.

7.2 ANONYMOUS REMAILER SERVICES

The best-known remailer service is Hushmail (https://www.hushmail.com/). Hushmail solves several of the issues noted with temporary e-mail services by using HTTPS, and it encrypts your messages while they are stored. Also, if you send e-mail to another Hushmail user, your message will remain encrypted—or you can encrypt your message with OpenPGP standards (otherwise, the message must be sent/received as plaintext, another vulnerability).

On the down side, however, Hushmail retains the ability to decrypt stored data in your account, and if it receives "an order that is legally enforceable under the laws of British Columbia, Canada, which is the jurisdiction where our servers are located" (from Hushmail's website), it will comply that order.

Hushmail is a big step up from most temporary/throwaway mail services, but it does not completely protect your privacy from a subpoena, or from an adversary that can get access to Hushmail's servers through a subpoena or any other method.

Hushmail is well established, and is used by corporations as well as being approved for HIPAA compliance to protect PHI ("protected health information" of medical patients in the US). If you access Hushmail strictly through Tor, and if you encrypt all your messages with a strong encryption program like GnuPG, Hushmail should be adequate for most users. However, keep in mind that any plaintext (unencrpyted) messages sent to your Hushmail account may be vulnerable to an adversary with access to the Hushmail servers.

7.3 ANONYMOUS E-MAIL THROUGH TOR

This is the option of setting up an account with an ordinary webmail service (like Gmail or Yahoo! Mail) through Tor. The key to this approach is that all access to the anonymous e-mail account must be through Tor: doing so insures that your physical location (traceable through the IP address you use to connect to the public Internet) is never exposed or connected to the e-mail account.

There are a few things you should look for in a webmail service:

- First, the service should support HTTPS, so that an adversary with the ability to monitor your local network will not have access to your plaintext passphrase or e-mails. Currently, both Gmail and Yahoo! support HTTPS.
- Next, you'll need to connect to the service and register an account, over Tor. Because of the way Tor works, some sites will interpret your connection as an attempt to attack their site. This may be due to receiving multiple requests from the same originating IP address (a Tor exit relay) in a short time. You can try switching identities with Vidalia, or just waiting a bit before retrying.
- Finally, you will want to find a mail service that requires neither an existing e-mail address nor a mobile phone number (for receiving SMS texts to authenticate you). If you give out your personal e-mail address or your personal phone number, you are no longer anonymous (not even a little bit).

At the moment (June 2013), Gmail requires either an e-mail address or a mobile phone number; Yahoo! sometimes requires an e-mail address, but not always—it depends on where the Tor exit node you are using is located.

Webmail service providers change their policies from time to time; until recently, Yahoo! mail did not support HTTPS, for example. Gmail requires either an existing e-mail address or a mobile phone number to register.

Sometimes, the information you must provide depends on where the service believes you are registering *from*. So for example, Yahoo! may require you to provide a mobile phone number, or not, depending on where Yahoo! thinks you are connecting from, based on the IP address of the exit relay you are using. If you are prompted for a mobile number, you can try again after requesting a different identity with Vidalia.

Given the current state of affairs, Yahoo! mail is probably the best option: it is possible to sign up without providing an existing e-mail address, it supports HTTPS, and it allows registering and accessing e-mail via Tor.

If you can create an anonymous e-mail address on Yahoo! or Gmail, you should never access that account except while using Tor (especially if you used Tor to set it up in the first place).

It may be tempting to use a throwaway or temporary account to sign up for Gmail, but keep in mind that if an adversary is monitoring your network connection, they will likely be able to see the plaintext of any messages sent to/from that throwaway account—with the result that they can fairly easily deanonymize your Gmail (or other) account through that initial temporary e-mail activity.

You should also remember that the contents and addressees of all your e-mail are more likely to contribute to your deanonymization than anything else. While your messages and addresses are protected by HTTPS when being sent to and from the server, you should be careful if you think your e-mail provider monitors the content of your account and act accordingly.

7.4 ANONYMOUS E-MAIL AS A TOR HIDDEN SERVICE

In an ideal world, you will know (and trust) someone who runs an e-mail server as a Tor hidden service. If you can get an account on such a server, you can be fairly confident that the only possible vulnerabilities will relate to the security skills of your mail server administrator and their ability to protect the integrity of the server and its contents from a determined adversary.

Using e-mail on a Tor hidden service protects your information and your identity, but only to the extent that you can trust the people who run the service to respect your privacy. With access to the mail server, an adversary would be able to read any plaintext messages you send or receive, as well as to see who you are corresponding with.

When using a public Internet mail service (like Yahoo! or Gmail) you are at least protected by dealing with a public corporation that follows rules and regulations about data privacy (though you are still vulnerable to adversaries who are able to coerce or corrupt officials or employees into revealing private information).

There is a webmail service called Tor Mail (see sidebar), but they are not affiliated with the Tor Project, and the people who run it have not made their identities known. It is probably a bad idea to use this service for sensitive information, even if you encrypt it, unless you also make sure that the people with whom you correspond are also using strongly anonymous e-mail addresses and all messages/files are encrypted prior to be transmitted.

More About Tor

Don't Trust Tor Mail

Currently, there is a webmail/mail service, called Tor Mail (http://tormail. org, also as a hidden service at http://jhiwjjlqpyawmpjx.onion/). TOR MAIL IS NOT AFFILIATED WITH THE TOR PROJECT—and it is far from clear who it IS affiliated with, so AVOID USING TOR MAIL.

Since it first surfaced, there have been various conjectures and guesses about who is behind Tor Mail, including suggestions that it is a project of the Russian security services—or perhaps someone else.

In other words, don't trust Tor Mail with anything—but particularly anything that is "interesting" or important to your safety. Even if you encrypt all your messages, there may be other vulnerabilities you are unaware of, especially since there is an assumption that anyone using Tor Mail is likely to be doing so to hide their activity. In other words, messages sent to or from Tor Mail are far more likely to contain sensitive information of some sort than typical messages sent over the public Internet.

7.5 ANONYMITY AND PSEUDONYMITY

An anonymous e-mail address becomes pseudonymous as soon as it is reused. That is because the anonymous tipster or whistle-blower who originally sent a single anonymous e-mail now becomes a particular anonymous tipster, the same one who sent the first tip. If the same source e-mail address is used, AND if the e-mail address can be used to send mail back, then the tipster should be particularly careful to protect his/her identity.

Pseudonymity may be sufficient or even preferable for some cases, especially where a whistle-blower or informant needs to exchange information, for example, where a whistle-blower needs to answer questions from a journalist or an informer needs to respond to requests from a law enforcement agency or official.

7.6 TIPS FOR E-MAILING ANONYMOUSLY

As has been noted earlier, your e-mail activities can make your anonymity very fragile. With e-mail, as with any other Internet service you use over Tor, you should try to keep in mind what data might be exposed by your different actions.

For example, if you are using an e-mail account anonymously, you should probably never use that account to send a message to your personal e-mail account—or to your friends, family, colleagues, or others that have real-world, nonanonymous connections to you.

Reading this book is a good start, as is doing more research. The EFF has a good overview to setting up and using e-mail anonymously called "A Tutorial on Anonymous Email Accounts" (https://www.eff.org/deeplinks/2012/11/tutorial-how-create-anonymous-email-accounts). Read on for some more tips and suggestions.

7.6.1 Protecting Anonymity While Using E-mail

The technical means to protect anonymity in e-mail are straightforward: connect to your e-mail account using Tor only, and only use a webmail site that supports HTTPS. However, you must also be aware that whoever has control over the e-mail server can access the plaintext of your messages—so encrypting your messages is a very good idea. However, even if you encrypt your messages, an adversary can determine who you are corresponding with (e-mail may be encrypted, but e-mail addresses are not), so again, care should be taken.

In addition to using Tor and HTTPS, to protect e-mail anonymity you may want to:

• Suggest your correspondents also use anonymous e-mail accounts. Your identity may be revealed by who you are communicating with, either through analysis ("Mr. X" is communicating with three of four partners in a business may cause an adversary to assume that Mr. X is the fourth partner), or through interrogation of the people with whom you exchange mail.

- Keep all messages free of identifying information, for example, who you are, where you will be at any specific time, your organization, your location, or anything else that might be a clue to your identity.
- Consider encrypting all messages. Doing so means that the e-mail service provider will not be able to scan your messages or decrypt them without your knowledge/permission. Allowing the service provider to encrypt your messages on your behalf means they can also decrypt your messages without your permission/knowledge.

7.6.2 Always Use Tor

Using Tor will effectively obscure your IP address from whatever server you are using to access/send mail. So, rule #1: always use Tor; rule #2: see rule #1.

Never access an anonymous e-mail account without Tor, because the e-mail provider can be presumed to be maintaining logs of all client accesses which include the IP address from which you are attempting to connect. If that IP address is a Tor exit node, your anonymity will be more likely to remain intact—but if you connect from any non-Tor node your account can be linked with that node.

There are many ways that access will reveal your identity:

- The access was from your personal computer in your own home, on your ISP account. Your anonymous account can now be linked to you because the mail service logs your IP address and can track you down through your ISP.
- The access was from a computer cafe where you had to show ID (for example, many public libraries require identification to use a PC). In this case, an investigator can get the client IP address from the e-mail provider, connect that to the library or cafe, and then request records of who was using computers at that location.
- Patterns of access can be used as well, for a good example see the Petraeus episode, where accesses to the "anonymous" Gmail account from different locations were correlated to individuals' travel records.

7.6.3 Use HTTPS, Always

Using Tor is necessary but not sufficient to maintain anonymity. Any data transiting the Tor network will be encrypted, but unless HTTPS is in use, messages will be transmitted in plaintext from the Tor exit node to the server (and from the server back to the user).

Using HTTPS Everywhere (https://www.eff.org/https-everywhere) is a good practice for any browsing, whether anonymous or not, and it is included with Tor Browser Bundle. So the key is to make sure you pick an e-mail provider that supports HTTPS access to your account.

7.7 STEP-BY-STEP: SETTING UP ANONYMOUS E-MAIL

One reasonable choice for setting up an anonymous e-mail account is Yahoo!, as it currently supports HTTPS access to e-mail, it allows signing up and accessing mail from the Tor network, and it does not (always) require an alternate e-mail account or phone number.

Setting up an e-mail account on Yahoo! that will not be easily linked to your identity is simple:

- Start the Tor Browser Bundle, make sure that you are configured for and using Tor, then go to Yahoo! (http://www.yahoo.com).
- You need to create a new Yahoo! ID, so go to a login page (via the Sign In or Mail buttons) and click "Create New Account."
- Fill out registration forms, being sure to *not* include an alternate e-mail address or phone number.

When filling out the registration forms, be careful to not use your real name, but also to use made-up information that will neither be linkable to you and that will be plausible. Keeping in mind the guideline that privacy loves company, selecting "Iraq–Saudi Arabia Neutral Zone" or "Wallis and Futuna" as your country may serve to make your account stand out. Far better to choose a populous country with high-Internet connectivity.

APPENDIX *A*

Validating Tor Software

A.1 VALIDATING TOR SOFTWARE WITH GNU PRIVACY GUARD

Gnu Privacy Guard (GnuPG) is the leading OpenPGP-compatible software for public key cryptography, which includes validating digital signatures. It is included by default on most Linux distributions, so acquiring a trusted version of Linux is the simplest and safest way to get the software necessary to validate signed downloads.

To validate a Tor download, follow these steps:

- Download the desired package (e.g., version of TBB appropriate for your system). The file will be named something like "TorBrowser-2.3.25-6-osx-i386-en-US.zip."
- Download the signature file, named something like "TorBrowser-2.3.25-6-osx-i386-en-US.zip.asc" (in other words, the same as the file downloaded, with the suffix ".asc" added). Simply clicking on the Tor Project website link labeled "sig" will display the signature on a new page (see illustration below). This page should be saved (or can be downloaded directly by holding down the Alt key while clicking it).
- Go to the system command line, change to the download directory, and enter the following command:

```
gpg --keyserver hkp://pool.sks-keyservers.net --recv-keys 0x63FEE659
```

This command downloads the signing key for Erinn Clark, the member of Tor Project responsible for signing the TBB downloads. (However, you should check the Tor Project website to be verify that this is still the case.) Doing this adds Erinn's public key to your GnuPG keyring. The next step is to verify the OpenPGP fingerprint for this key, by entering this command:

```
gpg --fingerprint 0x63FEE659
```

The system should return the following output:

```
pub   2048R/63FEE659 2003-10-16
Key fingerprint = 8738 A680 B84B 3031 A630  F2DB 416F 0610 63FE E659
uid                   Erinn Clark <erinn@torproject.org>
uid                   Erinn Clark <erinn@debian.org>
uid                   Erinn Clark <erinn@double-helix.org>
sub   2048R/EB399FD7 2003-10-16
```

If the second line (starting "Key fingerprint") does not match what is shown here (and on the Tor website), there is a problem. If it does match, enter the following command to verify the download:

```
gpg --verify *download-file*.zip.asc *download-file*.zip
```

The result (if the signature is verified) will look similar to the output shown in Figure A.1. Note that the WARNING line indicates that you have not explicitly taken the step of signing Erinn's key; it does not change the fact that the digital signature has been verified and the downloaded files are safe to use.

See Figure A.2 for an example of what the TBB digital signature looks like.

For more details about using GnuPG, see "Simple Steps to Data Encryption" (Loshin, 2013; http://www.amazon.com/gp/product/0124114830/ref=as_li_ss_tl?ie=UTF8&camp=1789&creative=390957&creativeASIN=0124114830&linkCode=as2&tag=internetstand-20)

A.2 VALIDATING TAILS DISTRIBUTION WITH GNUPG

To validate a Tails download, follow these instructions:

- Download the latest release of Tails, it will be named something like "tails-i386-0.17.2.iso."
- Download the signature file, which will be named something like "tails-i386-0.17.2.iso.pgp." Clicking on the Tails website link labeled "Cryptographic Signature" downloads the signature file.
- Go to the system command line, change to the download directory, and enter the following command:

```
gpg --keyserver hkp://pool.sks-keyservers.net --recv-keys 0xBE2CD9C1
```

```
$ gpg --verify TorBrowser-2.3.25-6-osx-i386-en-US.zip.asc
TorBrowser-2.3.25-6-osx-i386-en-US.zip
gpg: Signature made Thu Apr  4 23:21:29 2013 EDT using RSA key
ID 63FEE659
gpg: requesting key 63FEE659 from hkp server keys.gnupg.net
gpg: key 63FEE659: public key "Erinn Clark <erinn@torproject.org>"
imported
gpg: 3 marginal(s) needed, 1 complete(s) needed, PGP trust model
gpg: depth: 0  valid:  10  signed:   0  trust: 0-, 0q, 0n, 0m,
0f, 10u
gpg: next trustdb check due at 2014-11-12
gpg: Total number processed: 1
gpg:                  imported: 1  (RSA: 1)
gpg: Good signature from "Erinn Clark <erinn@torproject.org>"
gpg:                 aka "Erinn Clark <erinn@debian.org>"
gpg:                 aka "Erinn Clark <erinn@double-helix.org>"
gpg: WARNING: This key is not certified with a trusted signature!
gpg:          There is no indication that the signature belongs to
the owner.
Primary key fingerprint: 8738 A680 B84B 3031 A630  F2DB 416F 0610
63FE E659
```

Figure A.1 Output indicating a successful verification of a digital signature on the TBB download.


```
-----BEGIN PGP SIGNATURE-----
Version: GnuPG v1.4.12 (Darwin)

iQEcBAABAgAGBQJRXkM5AAoJEEFvBhBj/uZZQ5kIAOCPXWHC/Q5OsP79SnY5CEOk
qBub5XUg1ODdIZa127qNf31AlbbC0S9PdcLZPrm1HJyrT+Wyxc3QGS/oJgqKCx9/
WM7DCg+jsg4z4NU8Yk6U9oGpJaTw7/CkUptdlqvY/tNMGLs0erMy0yVwg/Kd01vk
3GCe8oeyNtUmq0K7D99ZrPjOjqUN7ShBo1+WyLWkKwJMvFopswnfJqDcPwUHqD/2
6JfFSGbJjT+jUU+1CwuFCuSIuCYSUckoEtVN0IfoDVs8MUuM38zJieJ8h17SPeo1
SOI66bWHK3/AwQ9no7bFGonf0TdY4Bt+CdZEjvoyp/DyzTh53J/24iYXrU7Pn+M=
=R5XS
-----END PGP SIGNATURE-----
```

Figure A.2 The digital signature file for a TBB download will look similar to this.

This command downloads the signing key for the Tails developers team, the entity responsible for signing the TBB downloads. However, you should check the Tails website to verify that this is still the case. Doing this adds the Tails developers' public key to your GnuPG keyring. The result will be something like that shown in Figure A.3.

```
$ gpg --keyserver hkp://pool.sks-keyservers.net --recv-keys
0xBE2CD9C1
gpg: requesting key BE2CD9C1 from hkp server pool.sks-keyservers.net
gpg: key BE2CD9C1: public key "Tails developers (signing key)
<tails@boum.org>" imported
gpg: 3 marginal(s) needed, 1 complete(s) needed, PGP trust model
gpg: depth: 0  valid:   1  signed:   0  trust: 0-, 0q, 0n, 0m, 0f,
1u
gpg: Total number processed: 1
gpg:                   imported: 1  (RSA: 1)
```

Figure A.3 Downloading the Tails developers' team signing key.

```
$ gpg --verify ~/Downloads/tails-i386-0.17.2.iso.pgp
~/Downloads/tails-i386-0.17.2.iso
gpg: Signature made Sun 07 Apr 2013 08:57:06 AM EDT using RSA key
ID BE2CD9C1
gpg: Good signature from "Tails developers (signing key)
<tails@boum.org>"
gpg:                   aka "T(A)ILS developers (signing key)
<amnesia@boum.org>"
gpg: WARNING: This key is not certified with a trusted signature!
gpg:         There is no indication that the signature belongs to
the owner.
Primary key fingerprint: 0D24 B36A A9A2 A651 7878  7645 1202 821C
BE2C D9C1
```

Figure A.4 Verifying the Tails ISO download file with its digital signature.

The next step is verifying the OpenPGP fingerprint for this key, by entering the command:

```
gpg --fingerprint 0xBE2CD9C1
```

The system should return output like this:

```
pub   4096R/BE2CD9C1 2010-10-07 [expires: 2015-02-05]
Key fingerprint = 0D24 B36A A9A2 A651 7878  7645 1202 821C BE2C D9C1
uid              Tails developers (signing key) <tails@boum.org>
uid              T(A)ILS developers (signing key) <amnesia@boum.org>
```

If the second line (starting "Key fingerprint") does not match what is shown here (and on the Tails website), there is a problem. If it does match, enter the following command to verify the download:

```
gpg --verify *download-file*.pgp *download-file*
```

The result (if the signature is verified) will look something like Figure A.4. Note that the WARNING line indicates that you have not explicitly taken the step of signing the Tails developers' key; the digital signature has been verified and the downloaded files are safe to use.

For more details about using GnuPG, see "Simple Steps to Data Encryption" (Loshin, 2013).

A.3 WHICH PGP KEYS SIGN WHICH PACKAGES

As of June 2013, the following keys are used to sign Tor and related packages (from the Tor Project website, at https://www.torproject.org/docs/signing-keys.html.en):

- Roger Dingledine (0x28988BF5 and 0x19F78451) or Nick Mathewson (0x165733EA, or its subkey 0x8D29319A) sign the Tor source code tarballs.
- Erinn Clark (0x63FEE659) signs the TBBs, Vidalia bundles, and many other packages. She signs RPMs with her other key (0xF1F5C9B5). Andrew Lewman (0x31B0974B, 0x6B4D6475) used to sign packages for RPMs, Windows, and OS X.
- Tor Project Archive (0x886DDD89) signs the deb.torproject.org repositories and archives.
- Tomás Touceda (0x9A753A6B) signs current Vidalia tarballs. Matt Edman (0x5FA14861) signed older Vidalia tarballs.
- Damian Johnson (0x9ABBEEC6) signs Arm releases.
- Mike Perry (0xDDC6C0AD) signs the Torbutton xpi.
- Robert Hogan (0x22F6856F) signs torsocks release tarballs.
- Alexandre Allaire (0x4279F297) and Sebastian Hahn (0xC5AA446D) sign Obfsproxy TBBs, and sometimes Sebastian signs the TBBs.
- The Tails team (0xBE2CD9C1) signs the Tails live system releases.
- Other developers include Peter Palfrader (0xC82E0039, or its subkey 0xE1DEC577) and Jacob Appelbaum (0xE012B42D).

The fingerprints for these keys are listed below:

```
Key fingerprint = B117 2656 DFF9 83C3 042B  C699 EB5A 896A 2898 8BF5
     uid                     Roger Dingledine <arma@mit.edu>


pub   4096R/19F78451 2010-05-07
Key fingerprint = F65C E37F 04BA 5B36 0AE6  EE17 C218 5258 19F7 8451
     uid                     Roger Dingledine <arma@mit.edu>
     uid                     Roger Dingledine <arma@freehaven.net>
     uid                     Roger Dingledine <arma@torproject.org>
     sub   4096R/BA694D6A 2011-04-26 [expires: 2012-05-08]


pub   3072R/165733EA 2004-07-03
Key fingerprint = B35B F85B F194 89D0 4E28  C33C 2119 4EBB 1657 33EA
     uid                      Nick Mathewson <nickm@alum.mit.edu>
     uid                      Nick Mathewson <nickm@wangafu.net>
     uid                      Nick Mathewson <nickm@freehaven.net>
     uid                      [jpeg image of size 3369]
     sub   3072R/8D29319A 2004-07-03
     sub   3072R/F25B8E5E 2004-07-03


pub   2048R/63FEE659 2003-10-16
Key fingerprint = 8738 A680 B84B 3031 A630  F2DB 416F 0610 63FE E659
     uid                     Erinn Clark <erinn@torproject.org>
     uid                     Erinn Clark <erinn@debian.org>
     uid                     Erinn Clark <erinn@double-helix.org>
     sub   2048R/EB399FD7 2003-10-16


pub   1024D/F1F5C9B5 2010-02-03
Key fingerprint = C2E3 4CFC 13C6 2BD9 2C75  79B5 6B8A AEB1 F1F5 C9B5
     uid                     Erinn Clark <erinn@torproject.org>
     sub   1024g/7828F26A 2010-02-03


pub   1024D/31B0974B 2003-07-17
Key fingerprint = 0295 9AA7 190A B9E9 027E  0736 3B9D 093F 31B0 974B
     uid                     Andrew Lewman <andrew@lewman.com>
     uid                     Andrew Lewman <andrew@torproject.org>
     sub   4096g/B77F95F7 2003-07-17


pub   4096R/6B4D6475 2012-02-29
Key fingerprint = 0291 ECCB E42B 2206 8E68  5545 627D EE28 6B4D 6475
     uid                     Andrew Lewman <andrew@torproject.org>
     uid                     Andrew Lewman <andrew@torproject.is>
     sub   4096R/BE713AC6 2012-02-29
```

```
pub     2048R/886DDD89 2009-09-04 [expires: 2014-09-03]
Key fingerprint = A3C4 F0F9 79CA A22C DBA8  F512 EE8C BC9E 886D DD89
    uid                    deb.torproject.org archive signing key
    sub     2048R/219EC810 2009-09-04 [expires: 2012-09-03]


pub     1024D/9A753A6B 2009-09-11
Key fingerprint = 553D 7C2C 626E F16F 27F3  30BC 95E3 881D 9A75 3A6B
    uid                    Tomás Touceda <chiiph@gmail.com>
    sub     1024g/33BE0E5B 2009-09-11


pub     1024D/5FA14861 2005-08-17
Key fingerprint = 9467 294A 9985 3C9C 65CB  141D AF7E 0E43 5FA1 4861
    uid                    Matt Edman <edmanm@rpi.edu>
    uid                    Matt Edman <Matt_Edman@baylor.edu>
    uid                    Matt Edman <edmanm2@cs.rpi.edu>
    sub     4096g/EA654E59 2005-08-17


pub     1024D/9ABBEEC6 2009-06-17
Key fingerprint = 6827 8CC5 DD2D 1E85 C4E4  5AD9 0445 B7AB 9ABB EEC6
    uid                    Damian Johnson (www.atagar.com)
<atagar1@gmail.com>
    uid                    Damian Johnson <atagar@torproject.org>
    sub     2048g/146276B2 2009-06-17
    sub     2048R/87F30690 2010-08-07


pub     1024D/DDC6C0AD 2006-07-26
Key fingerprint = BECD 90ED D1EE 8736 7980  ECF8 1B0C A30C DDC6 C0AD
    uid                    Mike Perry <mikeperry@fscked.org>
    uid                    Mike Perry <mikepery@fscked.org>
    sub     4096g/AF0A91D7 2006-07-26


pub     1024D/22F6856F 2006-08-19
Key fingerprint = DDB4 6B5B 7950 CD47 E59B  5189 4C09 25CF 22F6 856F
    uid                    Robert Hogan <robert@roberthogan.net>
    sub     1024g/FC4A9460 2006-08-19


pub     2048R/4279F297 2013-01-02
Key fingerprint = 97BB 9413 1873 FFD3 1331  64CC 7EB4 5C0A 4279 F297
    uid                    Alexandre Allaire
<alexandre.allaire@mail.mcgill.ca>
    sub     2048R/76D943F1 2013-01-02
```

```
    pub    4096R/C5AA446D 2010-07-14
Key fingerprint = 261C 5FBE 7728 5F88 FB0C  3432 66C8 C2D7 C5AA 446D
    uid                    Sebastian Hahn
    sub    2048R/A2499719 2010-07-14
    sub    2048R/140C961B 2010-07-14


    pub    4096R/C82E0039 2003-03-24
Key fingerprint = 25FC 1614 B8F8 7B52 FF2F  99B9 62AF 4031 C82E 0039
    uid                    Peter Palfrader
    uid                    Peter Palfrader <peter@palfrader.org>
    uid                    Peter Palfrader <weasel@debian.org>


    pub    4096R/BE2CD9C1 2010-10-07 [expires: 2015-02-05]
Key fingerprint = 0D24 B36A A9A2 A651 7878  7645 1202 821C BE2C D9C1
uid                Tails developers (signing key) <tails@boum.org>
uid                T(A)ILS developers (signing key) <amnesia@boum.org>
```

When Tor Downloads Are Blocked

This appendix explains some options for getting Tor software even when you are being blocked or filtered by an active adversary. Be sure to check the Tor Project website for more information or other options, or to get the most up-to-date workarounds for accessing the Tor network.

It is relatively easy for a nation-level firewall to block access to the Tor Project website (https://www.torproject.org). As noted in Chapter 4, the Great Firewall of China (GFC) has been observed to block access to URLs that contain the string torproject.org; however, mirrors (servers intended to "mirror" or be identical to the official Tor Project server) were accessible.

If the firewall/filter blocks access to the Tor Project server, you may still be able to get Tor software by accessing one of these mirrors. The trick is to find a way to discover good URLs for the mirrors, without being blocked/filtered.

Furthermore, it is possible for an adversary to block access to Tor Project mirrors, as well, in which case there is a mechanism by which you can request a copy of Tor by e-mail.

Finally, if all other mechanisms fail, you can get a copy of Tor from another Tor user—if you are careful.

And remember, in all case but especially when you have extra difficulty acquiring the Tor/Tails software, be sure to validate the digital signatures on the downloads.

B.1 TOR MIRRORS

The recommended way to get a list of Tor mirrors is to do a Google search on "tor mirrors" (see https://encrypted.google.com/search? q = tor + mirrors), and then look at the Google cache of the result (the top result is likely to be the Tor Project website's Tor Mirrors page at https://www.torproject.org/getinvolved/mirrors.html.en, which will likely be blocked by the national firewall).

To view the Google cache, click on the little upside-down green triangle next to the Tor Project's mirrors page URL (also in green), and choose "Cached." Google cached copy of that list will be displayed, including URLs to link directly to the mirror sites.

B.2 TOR VIA E-MAIL

The Tor Browser Bundle download is currently (as of June 2013) as much as 35 Mb; attaching a file of that size to an e-mail message can be difficult. However, it is possible to do it, and if you cannot reach the Tor Project website or any mirrors, you can get Tor via e-mail by sending a message to the address: `gettor@gettor.torproject.org` and including the word "help" in the body of the message. There may be other e-mail addresses ("aliases") that will produce the some responses; for the best and most current information, see the article, "GetTor e-mail autoresponder" (https://www.torproject.org/projects/gettor.html.en).

This e-mail address is an alias for an e-mail *robot* that responds with instructions (e.g., how to choose the operating system for which to download Tor Browser Bundle).

The GetTor autoresponder should respond to a "help" request with the following text (repeated in as many languages as have been translated), as shown in Figure B.1.

Some warnings and tips:

- *Use a Gmail or Yahoo! account to request Tor by e-mail.* These providers make it difficult to create large numbers of e-mail accounts, so by using one of them there is less risk (to the Tor Project) in responding to an e-mail request. The problem is that attackers wishing to disrupt Tor Project activities could generate large numbers of valid but unused e-mail addresses to deploy a denial of service (DoS) attack by swamping Tor e-mail servers with spurious requests.
- *If you have trouble getting a response, check the Tor Project bug tracker.* There are a lot of resources available to Tor users, and

Hello, This is the "GetTor" robot.

Thank you for your request.

I will mail you a Tor package, if you tell me which one you want.
Please select one of the following package names:

windows
macos-i386
macos-ppc
linux-i386
linux-x86_64
obfs-windows
obfs-macos-i386
obfs-macos-x86_64
obfs-linux-i386
obfs-linux-x86_64
source

Please reply to this mail, and tell me a single package name
anywhere in your reply. Here's a short explanation of what these
packages are:

windows:
The Tor Browser Bundle package for Windows operating systems.
If you're running some version of Windows, like Windows XP, Windows
Vista or Windows 7, this is the package you should get.

macos-i386:
The Tor Browser Bundle package for OS X, Intel CPU architecture.
In general, newer Mac hardware will require you to use this package.
Note that this package is rather large and needs your email provider
to allow for attachments of about 30MB in size.

macos-ppc:
This is an older installer (the "Vidalia bundle") for older Macs
running OS X on PowerPC CPUs. Note that this package will be
deprecated soon.

linux-i386:
The Tor Browser Bundle package for Linux, 32bit versions. Note that
this package is rather large and needs your email provider to allow
for attachments of about 30MB in size.

linux-x86_64:
The Tor Browser Bundle package for Linux, 64bit versions. Note that
this package is rather large and needs your email provider to allow
for attachments of about 30MB in size.

Figure B.1 What the response from the Tor Project GetTor e-mail robot looks like.

```
obfs-windows:
The Tor Obfsproxy Browser Bundle for Windows operating systems.
If you need strong censorship circumvention and you are running some
version of the Windows, like Windows XP, Windows Vista or Windows 7,
this is the package you should get.

obfs-macos-i386:
The Tor Obfsproxy Browser Bundle package for OS X, 32bit Intel CPU
architecture.

obfs-macos-x86_64:
The Tor Obfsproxy Browser Bundle package for OS X, 64bit Intel CPU
architecture.

obfs-linux-i386:
The Tor Obfsproxy Browser Bundle package for Linux, 32bit Intel CPU
architecture.

obfs-linux-x86_64:
The Tor Obfsproxy Browser Bundle package for Linux, 64bit Intel CPU
architecture.

source:
The Tor source code, for experts. Most users do not want this
package.

OBTAINING LOCALIZED VERSIONS OF TOR
=====================================
To get a version of Tor translated into your language, specify the
language you want in the address you send the mail to:

gettor+fa@torproject.org

This example will give you the requested package in a localized
version for Farsi (Persian). Check below for a list of supported
language codes.

Here is a list of all available languages:
gettor+ar@torproject.org:     Arabic
gettor+de@torproject.org:     German
gettor+en@torproject.org:     English
gettor+es@torproject.org:     Spanish
gettor+fa@torproject.org:     Farsi (Iran)
gettor+fr@torproject.org:     French
gettor+it@torproject.org:     Italian
gettor+nl@torproject.org:     Dutch
gettor+pl@torproject.org:     Polish
gettor+ru@torproject.org:     Russian
gettor+zh@torproject.org:     Chinese
```

Figure B.1 Continued

If you select no language, you will receive the English version.

BLOCKED ACCESS / CENSORSHIP
============================
If your Internet connection blocks access to the Tor network, you
may need a bridge relay. Bridge relays (or "bridges" for short) are
Tor relays that aren't listed in the main directory. Since there is
no complete public list of them, even if your ISP is filtering
connections to all the known Tor relays, they probably won't be
ableto block all the bridges.

You can acquire a bridge by sending an email that contains "get
bridges" in the body of the email to the following email address:

bridges@torproject.org

It is also possible to fetch bridges with a web browser at the
following url: https://bridges.torproject.org/

Another censorship circumvention tool you can request from GetTor
is the Tor Obfsproxy Browser Bundle. Please read the package
descriptions for which package you should request to receive this.

SUPPORT
=======
If you have any questions or it doesn't work, you can contact a
human at this support email address: help@rt.torproject.org

Figure B.1 Continued

sometimes things go wrong but are not noticed by Tor Project staff.
For example, the GetTor mail robot was not working correctly for
a period in spring 2013; a user reported this problem on wiki/bug
tracking site for Tor (https://trac.torproject.org/projects/tor) and it
was fixed soon after.

B.3 OTHER OPTIONS

If you know someone who uses Tor, you can ask them to give you a
copy of their software. This assumes that this is a person you actually
trust, a lot.

If you decide to go this route, you should be comfortable with this
person knowing that you are using Tor, and you should also be
comfortable that this is a person who has not been subverted, either
knowingly (e.g., by being coerced in some way) or unknowingly (e.g.,
by having their computers hacked to reveal their communications or
by having key logging software added to their Tor software).

If all Internet attempts (e.g., web, e-mail, Google cache/mirrors) fail, consider contacting the Tor Project via post or even by phone. See Appendix C for complete contact information, including e-mail addresses for support, postal address, phone number, SMS, and IRC options.

APPENDIX *C*

Getting Help and Finding Answers

The Tor Project, and Tails, are both free software released under what is known as the BSD 3-clause license (also known as "New" or "Revised" BSD). This is a very permissive open source license that allows redistribution as source code or binary software as long as the same copyright applies to the redistributed software.

This means anyone may use the software and its source code in any way they wish.

This means that if they run into any problems using the software, one of the things they can do is to study the source code, find the bug they want to remove or add the feature they want to use, and continue using the software.

Most users will not have the inclination, skills, or time to do this on their own, but because the projects are run as openly as possible, you do have access to Tor and Tails bug reports, pending bug fixes, mailing lists/IRC channels for discussing Tor and Tails, and the ability to make bug reports (bugs can be reported anonymously when using Tails, using the Whisperback application as described in Chapter 3).

Tor and Tails publish a huge amount of information on their websites, so this appendix lists some of the more important resources you may need for troubleshooting your Tor/Tails sessions.

C.1 TOR

Virtually everything that is done in the Tor Project is documented and published, usually on the Tor bug tracker/wiki.

C.1.1 Tor Bug Tracker/Wiki

The Tor Project maintains a combination bug tracker/wiki. This is a good page to bookmark because it provides an all-in-one resource for getting help when having trouble with Tor:

```
https://trac.torproject.org/projects/tor
```

This site is also accessible as a hidden service here:

```
http://vwp5zrdfwmw4avcq.onion/
```

C.1.2 Tor FAQ

The official main FAQ list is maintained here:

```
https://www.torproject.org/docs/faq
http://idnxcnkne4qt76tg.onion/docs/faq.html.en
```

There is another FAQ, published on the Tor bug tracker/wiki:

```
https://trac.torproject.org/projects/tor/wiki/doc/TorFAQ
```

Noted at the top of the page: "This FAQ is being migrated to General FAQ. The answers in this FAQ may be old, incorrect, or obsolete."

The emphasis should be on the word "may": many of these questions and answers were asked/answered years before, and some of the answers are now available only in the "official" FAQ noted above. However, many of these questions and answers are still useful and relevant—so if the official FAQ does not answer your question it may be worthwhile looking at this one.

C.1.3 Tor Documentation

Available here:

```
https://www.torproject.org/docs/documentation
http://idnxcnkne4qt76tg.onion/docs/documentation.html.en
```

For access to the "short manual" in all available languages:

```
https://www.torproject.org/docs/short-user-manual.html.en
```

C.1.4 Tor Hidden Server

To access the Tor website anonymously, use this pseudo-URL:

```
http://idnxcnkne4qt76tg.onion/
```

It should be noted almost all links on this page point to Tor hidden service pages. However, the link to the Tor bug tracker/wiki page is not a hidden service link.

The download links *do* point to pages on the Tor hidden server, so it is possible to download the Tor Browser Bundle from the hidden server (though the download will be noticeably slower than from the public site).

C.2 ABOUT THE TOR PROJECT

The Tor Project is a 501(c)(3) nonprofit based in US.

C.2.1 Contacting the Tor Project

The official address of the organization is:

> The Tor Project
> 969 Main Street, Suite 206
> Walpole, MA 02081-2972, USA

For more ways to contact someone at the Tor Project, see:

```
https://www.torproject.org/about/contact.html.en
```

Included on this page are suggestions for contacting Tor Project by:

- E-mail (for support and for mailing lists);
- Tor's microblogging account: https://identi.ca/torproject;
- IRC channels;
- SMS texting (experimental and not secure/anonymous);
- telephone (not secure/anonymous).

C.2.2 Tor Project People and Organizations

The people and organizations behind the Tor Project, both those who do the work and those who provide the funding, can be researched starting with these links:

- The 2012 Tor Project Annual Report (https://www.torproject.org/about/findoc/2012-TorProject-Annual-Report.pdf) gives an overview to the Tor Project and its activities during 2012, including summary of financial activity and project activity.

- Core Tor People (https://www.torproject.org/about/corepeople.html. en), an alphabetical list, with brief descriptions, of the people who are officially part of the Tor Project.
- Tor Sponsors (https://www.torproject.org/about/sponsors.html.en), sponsorship support is broken out into different levels characterized through the Linnaean classification of the common onion: at the highest level are those donors providing $1 million or more (*Magnoliophyta*, "flowering plants") down to those donating less than $50,000 (*Allium cepa*, "common onion"). Donors include Human Rights Watch, the Naval Research Laboratory, the National Science Foundation, and Google.
- Tor Financial Reports (https://www.torproject.org/about/financials. html.en), links to all available financial reports.

Printed and bound by CPI Group (UK) Ltd, Croydon, CR0 4YY

03/10/2024

01040423-0012